Innovate the Way You Were Designed To

Using Design Driven Development to Create
Products That Connect With Humans

Tom KraMer

authorHOUSE®

AuthorHouse™
1663 Liberty Drive
Bloomington, IN 47403
www.authorhouse.com
Phone: 833-262-8899

Published by AuthorHouse 07/27/2022

Library of Congress Control Number: 2022911167
ISBN: 978-1-6655-6240-9 (sc)
ISBN: 978-1-6655-6239-3 (hc)
ISBN: 978-1-6655-6238-6 (e)

Print information available on the last page.

Any people depicted in stock imagery provided by Getty Images are models, and such images are being used for illustrative purposes only. Certain stock imagery © Getty Images.

Scripture taken from the King James Version of the Bible.

This book is printed on acid-free paper.

Contents

Introduction vii

Section 1 How Were We Designed to Think?

Chapter 1   War Stories 1
Chapter 2   Buzz Words and Misconceptions 9
Chapter 3   Lessons Learned 17
Chapter 4   Left and Right Brain 30
Chapter 5   Linear vs. Divergent Thinking 38
Chapter 6   Humor and Creativity 47
Chapter 7   Brain Building 54

Section 2 A Path to Innovation

Chapter 8   A Broken Process 71
Chapter 9   Finding The Missing Process Parts 79
Chapter 10   Process Is Wrong, Right? 83
Chapter 11   Design-Driven Development 87
Chapter 12   Phase Descriptions 92
Chapter 13   Success Statistics 144

References 153

Introduction

Diving In with My Eyes Closed

As a young man, I was plunged, quite by accident, into the holistic union of art, design, and engineering. As I aimlessly transitioned from high school to college, I had no real clue as to how I was going to make a living. For some reason, that did not stop me from moving into my own place when I was nineteen years old, with no money, an old broken-down car, and a minimum-wage job working on the floor of a printing factory.

At this point, I had been out of high school for a year, and I had already determined that I was going to go to college in the fall, even though I did not have one penny to pay for it. This decision had been made as I sat in front of a metal die-stamping machine at my previous minimum-wage job. The repetitive booming rhythm of the machine droning on for eight hours a day every day seemed to be chanting repeatedly to me, *I have to go to college, I have to go to college.* So what was I going to go to college for?

In high school, the subject I loved the most was art. I excelled at it, and I loved all aspects of it. I had made album covers for the school orchestra, created paintings as Christmas presents for my family, and bribed my way out of trouble with the dean of students by supplying him with a large print of one of my engravings that he fancied for his living room wall. By the time I was a senior, I was being consistently employed to do oil portraits for friends and relatives. Favors and honor were the most common forms of payment. This helped me realize that a starving artist was not going to be a reliable means of support for the future, and my parents made sure I was well aware of that fact.

The most closely related occupation that I could think of to the art world was something called a *commercial artist*. The term *graphic designer* had not become well known at that point in time, so people who used their artistic talents for income were known as commercial artists. I liked this because it sounded respectable to my parents and was a career that they could get behind—although this was only true after they let go of their long-held dream that I would become a doctor.

So that fall, I headed off to the Minneapolis College of Art and Design (MCAD) in Minneapolis, Minnesota, to get a commercial art degree. It was to be a four-year liberal arts bachelor's degree in art and design. MCAD was a small private college with a high tuition, but I was convinced that getting loans for the entire bill and making monthly payments for fifteen years after graduation was better than pounding metal parts out of a stamping machine for the rest of my life. This was an extremely frightening decision at the time, but one that proved to be remarkably fortunate.

This entrance into the art world was my wormhole into design and engineering, although I had no clue at the time where it would actually take me. My freshman year consisted of a lot of general classes like color theory, figure drawing, and art history. But during the preparation for my sophomore year, something happened that would change my trajectory dramatically.

I was registering for my sophomore classes, but remember, back then there was no such thing as the internet. Al Gore may have had it imagined in his mind, but he had not executed it at this point. The world was still waiting on him for that gift to humanity. So we had to stand in lines to register for classes—long lines waiting to get to a table where people sat with paper and pencils and wrote our names on the class lists that we selected.

The problem with this class registration method was that many of the classes filled up before you got up to the table, and you would have to make an impromptu decision about a replacement class. This was no easy task for those who cannot react quickly under pressure. In fact, the person who turned out to be my best friend from college was the girl standing next to me in line, who lost all her class selections by the time we got to the table.

When asked what classes she wanted to take, she just started crying, pointed at me, and blurted out through her sobbing and tears, "Just give me what he has!" We had every class together that year and developed a deep friendship that endures to this day.

As I was haggling at the registration table over lost elective classes, I realized I was going to have to find a substitute for one of my desired electives. At that point, I was ready to pick anything just to get out of the line. I perused the course list and found an elective that was not filled: "Industrial Design." I had never heard of this, and it sounded kind of boring, but it was open and I took it. I was unaware at the time of the significance of this event.

Our first assignment in the industrial design class involved coming up with an idea for some kind of device, figuring out how it would work, and making a prototype of the final design with our own hands. For a kid who had played with Legos until he was fifteen years old, this sounded more like a fun, free-time activity than college study. This was the kind of thing my buddies and I did all the time in our high school years in our basements. We had conceived of and made a variety of archery devices, bombs, automatic bed-making devices, vehicles, boats, rafts, booby traps, and forts—all the things teenage boys' minds are capable of conceiving of in their own little world.

Needless to say, I was thrilled with the assignment. I remember asking the professor during the first class, "Do you mean to tell me that I can get a job doing this kind of thing, and someone will pay me for it?" I was in disbelief.

He seemed to think I was an idiot for asking. He was from Germany, and industrial design and German engineering were common aspects of life for him.

I took to the class like a fish to water and had a fun, wild ride immersing myself in the world of creativity, innovation, design, engineering, manufacturing, design theory, and design methodology. The desire to understand how people might use the devices we were conceiving of inspired me to delve into the social sciences at the college, where we learned about behavioral science, psychology, ethnography, philosophy, ergonomics, semantics, and human factors.

In the end, it took me six years to get through a four-year

undergraduate degree program in industrial design, mainly because halfway through I had to increase the hours at my job to full time just to stay financially afloat. Nevertheless, five years after I made the decision to change my major to industrial design, I graduated with a 3.5 GPA and a truckload of debt.

The Real World

In many professions, when students are sent out into the real world from college, they are tossed out like sheep among wolves. I felt the same fear that most graduates do when they are released into the wild. For the first twelve months after graduation, I could not find anyone who was hiring locally, but I kept busy by picking up a few freelance customers whose design work I did in the evenings from my home office in my basement.

My first big shock concerning the real world came while I was working on one of those projects. After learning from my German gestalt-esque college professor about the cohesive nature of design and the way design concepts and methods are used throughout the entire product development process in a symbiotic and nurturing way, I expected that surely all the large manufacturing companies out there would be operating this way. It was quite a shock to me when I felt like it was just me. When I sat in conference rooms with managers and engineers at my customers' locations, I would inevitably be amazed by the complete lack of process that took these holistic concepts into account.

In hindsight, I see that I owe many thanks to my professor for teaching me to think that way. I assumed if I learned it in college, that must be the way things were done in the real world. Not so.

I'll never forget one of those times on a project when I was tasked with coming up with some concepts for a simple consumer device. I used some of the ideation methods we learned in class and developed a few concepts in a simple-to-complex order according to the design criteria I'd developed through investigation. This was what I considered standard methodology based on my training.

The results were quite humorous. The people at the Fortune 500 company I was doing this work for did not expect to see concepts that solved the problem in functional ways that were different from their single line of thinking. They had made the mistake of beginning their creative process with an idea, and then began to develop the details of that idea until they ran into a wall that prevented it from being manufactured at an acceptable cost. This was why they'd called in reinforcements.

I had been given a week and tasked with coming up with a way to make the concept workable. When I showed them several concepts that achieved the desired results with some different functional methods, there was silence in the room for quite some time. Then the engineering manager spoke up and said, "We didn't expect you to have working concepts at this point. We are going to have to sit on these concepts for a couple of months before we show them. If we show them to upper management now, there is no way they will believe that we came up with these working solutions in a week."

Apparently, things took a lot longer in a large corporation with a lot of people and no real development method that harnessed the power of creative thinking. Imagine that.

As my career grew over the years, I began to see the need to capture our way of design thinking (we called it *design mindfulness* back then, as the term *design thinking* had not been popularized yet) and lay it out in a step-by-step process that would include all of those creative, hard-to-do, minimally understood tasks in a proper order. This would first be used to clarify our design process for our team, but then eventually to illustrate a product development methodology to our customers that became what we call the Design Driven Development® Process or D3 Process®.

In the following chapters, I want to first share with you what I consider natural processes regarding creativity and thinking in humans, and the consequences of abiding by these principles or abandoning them. Then I will attempt to detail out the Design Driven Development® Process in simple enough terms to be understood, but with enough complexity in the description that it can be used successfully.

To all you Lego-building art geeks, I hope you enjoy the ride.

Part One

How Were We Designed to Think?

Chapter 1

War Stories

We were sitting in the conference room. Rain was pouring down onto the windows, and the pitter-pat of the drops was all that broke the deafening silence. Around the table were nine people from a large medical-device company, and I was just a consultant rookie who was learning the ropes and keeping my mouth shut.

The VP of marketing had just finished informing all of the other VPs and their teams that their medical device was losing market share fast to a competitor's new device, and at the rate they were losing, they would be selling zero units within three years' time.

As I look back on the events that followed that meeting, I now realize that a process was followed that I did not recognize back then—a process that I now see all too often.

Earlier that year, the VP of marketing got someone from his team to gather some voice-of-customer data. This was one of the leading salespeople, and he had a lot of connections with users, so he queried them about what they wanted to see in a new device. This information was later brought back to the engineering team, and they proposed an idea for a new device that would seem to function in the way users were asking for. The team spent six months engineering this device, and by that time had a rough feasibility model put together.

It was butt-ugly. Marketing was giving engineering pressure to make it look different with the hope of not losing adoption in the market due to a bad impression by the users. The product was also difficult to handle and use correctly.

The engineering manager had called us in as a design consultant to make a better-looking handle for the device. As we began to get involved, we started to propose other methods of use and function for the device, some of which were novel and promising and could potentially reduce procedure time, patient pain, and cost. We suggested a couple of these concepts, and here we were sitting in the conference room with the deafening silence.

As I gazed across the table at the engineering manager, I was confused by the silence. The concepts we had come up with the prior week, prototyped, and just showed them seemed good. Why was no one saying anything?

Finally, the engineering manager cleared his throat and spoke. "Look, we have had a team of guys on this for six months and have gone through most of our budget. There is no way we are going to turn around now and start over in another direction. Perhaps these ideas can be used for a next-gen version later."

Unfortunately, that company never got a chance to implement a next-gen version. The version they released was dismal in the market, and they killed it as a product because it was costing far more than it was generating.

I learned some valuable lessons in those early years, and this experience was among the most memorable for me. That company and the company I mentioned previously, which opted to take a two-month wait in development, are both well established Fortune 500 companies with names anyone would recognize. What was astounding to me at the time was the huge amount of time-wasting and budget-spending that was going on.

It may not be such a bad thing to have a large product-development budget if the project is complex and intricate, but it is quite another to have that large budget get spent doing things over a second and third time late in the development timeline when a proper methodology could successfully accomplish those tasks early on. And the fact that management was conditioned to believe it took this long was tragic, as the employees would live up (or down) to that expectation to make their lives a little easier.

It seemed that the role of an outsourced design and development group was more important than I'd known when I started in the business. The ability to move quickly and adhere to an efficient process was something that seemed difficult for the large companies but was second nature for us. This was from necessity. People hired us to do things quickly and efficiently. If we wanted the work, we had to make good on that promise, and as a couple of young, hungry guys who'd just started their own consulting firm and were trying to make ends meet, we put everything we had into it.

I remember another project experience with a company that will remain unnamed. It is another situation that seems to vividly illustrate the point that following a cohesive process in the real business world only happens when the stars align. This one, however, is an example of success, not failure

This was not a Fortune 500 Company. It was a small start-up with four very smart guys: a research scientist, an electrical engineer, a mechanical engineer, and a successful serial CEO. They had conceived of an idea for a minimally invasive surgery technique that would save both physician and hospital time and money, while simplifying the procedure for both the physician and the patient, and reducing recovery time and side effects. They also believed their new technology would increase the effectiveness of the procedure and lead to more positive outcomes. Pretty exciting stuff.

They had built a Rube Goldberg device that seemed to prove the feasibility of their idea. Now they needed to convert it into a form that could be used in early clinical trials to get a deeper assurance that the technology was for real. Time to call in the designers.

What was wrong with this picture? Well, using the word *wrong* may be the problem here. There was nothing wrong with the picture. But the process that I'd learned in college was not being followed. Or was it?

Here is how the process was supposed to go according to my German "gestalt" professor:

1. You found a need for a device to solve a problem for a user.
2. You found all the small ancillary needs associated with that need and created a device criteria list based on them.

3. You brainstormed and deepened exploration through ideation to create many options for meeting that need with potential device solutions.
4. You then down-selected and came up with a single concept that espoused all of the most acceptable features to meet all the needs.
5. You engineered all the details to create a production-ready user device, after making several consecutive prototypes along the way that ranged from simple to complex, and tested them with users.

This was not the process that was followed by my four friends at the start-up company with a minimally invasive surgical device concept. They had a mechanical idea for how to make the thing work with a hypothesis that it would have the desired effect, and then they created the contraption that would show if they were right or wrong.

Who knew at this point if it would meet the user's needs? Who knew if it would be manufacturable at a price point that would make sense in the market? Nobody. It was a hope and a dream on a wing and a prayer by the founder, who, based on his extensive experience in the field, coupled with his understanding of the current devices, their complexity, their cost, and their effectiveness, had a good, educated gut feeling that it would be possible.

Here is how that project played out: We took the mechanical guts of the technology they had put together and created an early version of the device that seemed to at least come close to meeting user needs. Early studies were performed with this device, and we learned a lot about what users really felt, what was working well, and what needed refinement. We then created an improved device, performed user studies, and created a usability engineering file. European clinical trials were performed with this device, and a final refined version was created from the learnings that became the eventual commercial version receiving FDA approval, with a subsequent acquisition by a large Fortune 500 company. Super success story.

The point I want to make here is that the proper design and development procedure was followed in this case, even though it doesn't look like it. From the outside design eye looking in, it seems like a "shoot first and ask questions later" approach. In reality, my professor's procedure as described above was followed, but in a way that used prototypes that were developed and refined in parallel with the development of the actual functionality of the technology. To us, it felt like we were writing reports on historical data, but in reality, the process was just occurring over a longer period, with larger swings at each phase of the process.

The downside? Quite a bit of time and money was raised and spent over the course of the project because of this. Could the process have been shortened? Potentially. Every situation is different and calls for wisdom on the part of the developers. However, it seems that a process that generally outlines activities in the most profitable order applies to all situations, even if there are unique circumstances. These circumstances just need to be worked into the process. We will see how to do this in the following chapters.

Your Brain Was Designed to Solve Problems

Much of the ability to be successful in creative mental activities comes from an understanding of the parts of the brain and how they were designed to work. One important thing to understand is that the part of your brain responsible for creative problem-solving is in your right hemisphere. We often believe that engineers are left-brained people, and when they have mechanical or functional problems to solve, they use their superhuman left-brain superpower to do it. This couldn't be further from the truth.

Our team was attending a seminar from the Institute for Brain Potential, and they revealed that the part of the brain that gets the humor of a joke is the same part that solves problems, and it is on the right side. This means that exercising the right side of the brain with humor, art, and other types of abstract thinking could strengthen the part of the brain responsible for creative problem-solving (because it is neuroplastic) and make us more creative thinkers.

To me, this meant we were right on track, because we as humans

5

were designed to have fun *and* solve creative problems, both of which were the bedrock of the culture we developed at Kablooe.

Prior to learning this nugget of truth, I had spent a lot of time at conferences, lectures, and seminars trying to convince left-brained engineers that they could be creative people. Some of them were excited by that challenge, but the majority were skeptical. It seemed many wanted to hang on to their left-brained tendencies as a badge of honor. I wanted them to know that the creative parts of the process shouldn't be left to the designers only—that the process was holistic, and if you participated in product development, you should be participating in the creative work too. This is exactly what my professor taught us in college.

I never had much luck with this argument, however, because I was fighting two strong forces. First, the corporate society that many engineers lived in practiced pigeonholing workers in a single task area, and the engineers were used to it. There is a certain amount of security that comes with the idea that you only have to be responsible for one thing and nothing more, and many engineers did not want to give up that security for the uncertainty of being responsible for something creative that cannot be defined.

The second obstacle was lack of evidence. Most people were familiar with Meyers-Briggs and similar tests that told us what kind of personalities we had, and most people automatically linked a strong behavior of theirs to a stronger side of their brain. I would tell them that they have this thing called the corpus callosum, and it connected the two halves of the brain. Unless it was severed, they could use both halves. Even though this made sense to me, the argument was largely ineffective in convincing engineers who were used to evidence-based decisions that one side of their brain was not dominant over the other.

My breakthrough came in 2013 when a study done at the University of Utah showed that personality types had nothing to do with one side of your brain being stronger than the other. This gave me clinical evidence to back up my existing claims that anyone can have access to that right side, no matter what their personality is like, and be a creative problem-solver.

There is other evidence as well. Sir Ken Robinson gave a TED talk—the most viewed TED talk in history—that walked through a twenty-year study investigating the creative thinking abilities of a group of children who grew from age five to twenty-five during the study. Almost all of the five-year-olds were able to show creative-thinking abilities. But as they aged through the educational system, those abilities eroded to nearly nothing by age twenty-five.

The salient point here was that they *had* those abilities at one time in their life. If they once had a strong functional right brain, the argument that they can't have one now disappears. It is then replaced with the question of how to get it back, and as we all know, nothing physically changes in our bodies without three major things: practice, practice, and practice.

If we look back in history, we can easily find clues to support this thinking. At the roots of the Greek philosophies that founded our current Western culture, we see four major areas of philosophical thought by the likes of Socrates, Plato, and Aristotle: metaphysics, epistemology, axiology, and logic. All of these were taught as equally important in order to create a society of rational thinkers.

On today's campuses, it would be out of place to think that the study of axiology (beauty, art, etc.) is part of becoming a rational-thinking engineer, yet the founders of our culture thought it to be so. And perhaps they were on to something, knowing that the part of the brain that appreciates art and beauty is the same part responsible for creative problem-solving. Socrates didn't have access to the brain scans we do now, yet through observation and study, he saw this to be true.

Out of this kind of holistic training have come some of the greatest thinkers of all time. The most obvious example is Leonardo da Vinci, who was an inventor, engineer, artist, musician, and writer. It is amazing to see the work he was able to do employing both sides of his brain. With examples like that, why would we ever want to pigeonhole ourselves into a limited set of activities designed to only use one side of the brain?

Linear Thinking is Not Creative

Part of the problem that Sir Ken Robinson was identifying in his study was the setup of our educational system. It seems that during the industrial revolution, the assembly-line mentality began to seep into our school system and our methods of teaching youth. He compared it to running kids through a factory of memorization that pumps out people who memorized facts they needed to know for a test on the other end.

In doing so, we remove the need for a lot of creative thinking. Rote memorization uses a part of your brain that has nothing to do with creativity. We worked to strengthen the memorization part of youngsters' brains, and in the process let the creative-thinking part atrophy.

Chapter 2

Buzz Words and Misconceptions

The world of product design and development is filled with many different kinds of players. The designers and engineers are at the core of the field, but there are so many other types of people involved. There are usability/human-factors experts, ethnographers, researchers, quality-management-system experts, user-interface designers, user-experience designers, marketing people, branding experts, investors, project managers, program managers, manufacturing people, assembly experts, salespeople, and corporate leaders. If you are working with a medical device, there are also clinical folks, reimbursement experts, regulatory experts, clinical experts, and testing people.

Because there is such a varied array of people involved in product development, terminology can get thrown around and misunderstood, having different meanings for different groups of people. So it seems wise at this point to lay out the definitions for some of those terms, since we will be discussing them here. The idea will not be to say that these are the only definitions, or even the correct definitions. It is just to give a common understanding as we discuss these issues.

Innovation

The first word to tackle is *innovation*. Boy, talk about a word that has been overused to the point of diluting and polluting its meaning.

I have a couple of definitions for innovation that I like to draw upon. Understanding these definitions will help frame all our discussions about innovation henceforth. Even though Webster's defines innovation as "1: The introduction of something new" and "2: a new idea, method, or device: NOVELTY," this seems supremely weak. The following are my two favorite definitions:

- *Innovation* only exists after the new concept is accepted and adopted by the market and generates revenue for the company. (Anonymous)
- "Research is the transformation of money into knowledge. *Innovation* is the transformation of knowledge into money. Geoffrey Nicholson, 3M" (Soon, 2013)

These definitions will sound almost sacrilegious to the creative person, because they both talk about money. Isn't pure art inherently creative regardless of who sees it or how anyone else may value it? Yes. This is true of art. But innovation and art are not the same things

The reason I like these definitions is simply because if you adhere to them, you have to actually make your innovation work in the real world. You can't just come up with something you think is a creative idea and call yourself innovative. Anyone can do that. Coming up with a creative idea that is executable in the real world is an entirely different thing, and those who can make that happen truly are innovative. All of the others are eventually forgotten or never recognized.

These definitions of innovation will help us have a common knowledge so that when we discuss the subject, we know that the endgame is to have a result that is executable in the real world, thereby having a positive effect on lives and situations. This is the true aim of the innovator.

Design Thinking

Another common buzzword term is *design thinking.* (Wikipedia 2022) talks about design thinking in terms of breaking problems down into their various parts, then synthesizing positive attributes of possible solutions into one. This involves things like divergent and convergent thinking, user-centeredness, left- and right-brain thinking, empathy, brainstorming, and prototyping.

Although many people today believe that the founders of the design firm IDEO are the creators of the term *design thinking*, its history can actually be traced back to the 1960s. To give credit where it is due, however, the leaders of IDEO did popularize the term in its currently understood form. Their definition of design thinking is "a human-centered approach to innovation that draws from the designer's toolkit to integrate the needs of people, the possibilities of technology, and the requirements for business success." (Brown 2009)

In short, it is what our beloved German professor taught us to do in industrial design school: find a human need, create a solution or solutions, and bring the solution into reality in a tangible, workable way for those with the need. This meant, according to our professor, that when we thought of the needs of the user, we also had to understand the business and manufacturing needs, and to investigate technology and methods for achieving the best possible solution to the problem surrounding the fulfillment of these needs. It seems very logical, and surprising that anyone would try to solve a problem or come up with an innovative solution without doing those things. However, things always seem obvious once you are exposed to them; prior to that exposure, such concepts can be completely obscured without you realizing it. Remember my earlier experiences as an industrial designer freelancing for large companies.

If I was at a family reunion and my aunt (who is a farmer) asked me what *design thinking* was, I would probably try to sum it up by telling her that it is trying to solve a problem by first thinking about the needs of the person who is in the situation and making sure those needs get met in our solution to the problem. The understanding for those of us who are embarking on the development process is that this "meeting of needs" employs all of the things that Wikipedia and IDEO describe above, but most importantly adds "do whatever is necessary to discover and understand user needs, then employ means of developing concepts to meet those needs, testing them with those users, refining them for the better, and retesting until we are confident that we have a design that will be accepted by those users."[1]

Fuzzy Front End

Another phrase we often hear thrown around in the design and development community is *fuzzy front end*. I have a lot of fun with this one because I believe it is rooted in the fear that comes from lack of knowledge when working on endeavors outside of one's own field of study. Let me explain.

Pretend for a moment that you are a barber. You cut men's hair in a very manly, old-fashioned barber shop. You had one regular customer who made monthly visits, but he got a promotion at work, and now every time he comes in for a haircut, he also asks for a pedicure. You want to turn down the request and tell him to see a specialist.

But what if the owner of the barbershop required you to meet the patron's request? You would experience some fear of correctly executing the activity. Without researching proper methods or getting proper pedicure training, you would most likely develop a way of doing pedicures that was uniquely your own but most likely also ineffective or ill-advised. Over time, you might perhaps give the task of giving pedicures in your barbershop chair a name, like *mystery foot massage* or *toe tingle treatment*. You would be naming the procedure something based on your experience of it, which came from fear due to lack of training. So it is with the fuzzy front end.

Industrial designers and human-factors engineers are trained to engage in certain activities at the beginning of the product development process. These activities set the stage for coming up with all the requirements that will dictate the development of device details further down the road. Most other types of engineers have no formal training in these activities, so they begin their work with a formal set of requirements. If you were to give these engineers the task of finding

---

[1] . My definition of design thinking, formerly called *design mindfulness* by the leadership at Kablooe Design in the early 1990s.

12

those requirements without telling them how to do it, it might seem like quite a fuzzy process to them.

This is not true just of engineers; imagine the same situation for people in business, finance, and other corporate roles who are on the same development journey. The process would seem fuzzy, and they would be afraid of spending large amounts of time and money on the project with nothing to show for it because concept prototypes are developed much later in the process.

When design thinking began to gain popularity in the late '90s and early 2000s, these engineers and corporate people began to understand that they needed to have a more fully developed set of requirements that went beyond the mere mechanical/electrical function of their device. Without understanding how to do it themselves, they rightfully turned over the task of developing early requirements to the industrial designers and human-factors engineers. These folks did their work, but the tasks were mostly out of view of the corporate people and engineers, and thus there was a lack of understanding from corporate and engineering about what was going on in those early tasks. Thus it was dubbed the fuzzy front end.

Fuzzy front end basically means that early in the development process, not all of the requirements are clear, and few people know what to do about it. But forward progress needs to be made to hit deadlines, so there is a push into the unknown to see what will be discovered. This is the stuff of explorers, not builders.

Human-Factors Engineering

Human-factors engineering (also known as *usability engineering*) is an activity that employs the tools of the human-factors discipline throughout the development process. Human factors can be thought of as a discipline that quantifies human performance, capabilities, and limitations. A more commercially relatable definition is "an applied science that coordinates the design of devices, systems, and physical working conditions with the capacities and limitations of the worker." (Dictionary.com, 2022). It is also referred to at times as *ergonomics* and *human-factors engineering*.

As is the case in almost any industry, people from outside the discipline misuse the terms and attach incorrect meanings to them. Often, someone who is involved in the product-development process, but whose training is outside the discipline of human factors or industrial design, will be thinking about ergonomics, aesthetics, or the semantics of a visual language for the device being developed and refer to these attributes as human factors. These are all things that industrial designers take into account in their work, but they are not human factors.

I have found that the easiest and best way to classify something as a human-factors activity is to ask if it involves a capability or limitation of the user of the device or system being developed. If so, it falls into the category of human-factors engineering. This does not have to be limited to the physical aspects of the user but also includes the mental capacities, such as memory, understanding, and comprehension.

There is an entire discipline of human-factors engineering that engages in activities throughout the entire product-development cycle and is controlled by industry standards and guidance, such as IEC 62366 and ISO 14971, as well as HE75 from the FDA. It is important to note that this discipline is commonly referred to as human-factors engineering in the United States but is most commonly referred to as *usability engineering* in Europe and other parts of the world, as evidenced in the European standard IEC 62366.

Empathy

Empathy is not sympathy. Webster's dictionary includes in its definition of empathy the idea of "vicariously experiencing the feelings, thoughts, and experience of another." Dictionaries get very precise in trying to illustrate the difference between these two words for us, but the simplest way for me to understand it is to remember that *sympathy* is feeling sorry for someone—"Boy, it sure would be bad to be in her situation; she must really be hurting"—and empathy is feeling what someone else feels—"I know how you feel; I completely wrecked my car in an accident too."

Why is this important in product design and learning how to innovate? Because as we saw earlier, much of the success of an innovative effort revolves around the intended user's needs and making sure these are met. What better way to shortcut that process than by having those who are designing and engineering the innovative solution be those who actually feel what the user feels and understand what the user understands. This flows directly into our next definition.

User-Centered Design

There is not a lot of ambiguity around this term, and very little misinterpretation. However, I felt it was important enough to mention just so we can be sure that there is a common understanding as we apply the term to our innovation efforts.

The best way to bring a deeper meaning to this term might be to look at other forms of development that may be centered on other things. For instance, someone may want to put most of the focus of their development on technology. Forget about users and whether or not they will warm up to your invention. It may be that you need to get the darn technology to work, and without that, you have nothing.

Many development efforts start that way. An example could be a minimally invasive surgical technique that uses a new form of energy to ablate tissue inside the human body. If this is the core invention that is patented, then technology and feasibility studies have to be done first to make sure it actually works. User-centered design follows closely behind. Sometimes it follows so closely that the developers engage in user-centered design as soon as there is a reasonable glimpse of hope that the technology may actually work. This may be important, because early user testing is on the horizon, and you don't want to potentially incur poor testing results only because your users had trouble successfully completing the required tasks.

User-centered design, then, can easily be thought of as designing and developing in such a way that the first priority and activity is understanding the needs of the user of the device or system, and making sure these needs are met in the final solution. Aside from an untested technology development effort as described above, I believe that user-centered design is the bedrock of innovation, and the best and smartest way to approach an innovation challenge.

Design Research

I use the term *design research* a lot during the process when I am involved in a development project. I didn't invent the term, but according to Wikipedia, it initially referred more to research into the process of designing things, and later morphed into a term including the research that is done during the design process to inform the process. (Wikipedia, 2021). The latter is how I am referring to it in this book.

Design research is an umbrella term, and it mostly refers to any part of the development process that gathers information that will inform and affect the design of the device or system. This can include a myriad of activities, many of which we will touch on later in this book.

Usability

The last term I want to give a brief explanation of is *usability*. This one will be short because, as we saw earlier, it can be synonymous with human-factors engineering. The only point worth making here is that while usability engineering is mostly talked about as a discipline, just as human-factors engineering is, the term *usability* by itself is often misinterpreted to mean the same things that the term *human factors* is misinterpreted as meaning.

When people use the word *usability*, sometimes they are referring to the object's visual appeal or its shape. Other times, they may be referring to its acceptability in the marketplace. In this book, I will stick with the strict definition of referring to the investigation into solving dilemmas that are directly related to the capabilities and limitations of the intended user of the device or system.

Chapter 3

Lessons Learned

Things aren't always as we perceive them to be. Oftentimes we think the people "behind closed doors" are doing the things we think they are doing... solving problems, making discoveries, and creating products, policies and paradigms that are in the best interest of our products, companies, and selves. This perpetuates the myth of the greater "they" that we too often acquiesce to with the belief that someone else is handling things and doing everything right.

We Don't Innovate

In 2006, medical-device giant Boston Scientific paid about $27 billion for Guidant Corporation, a manufacturer of cardiovascular medical devices. Later in 2015, Medtronic paid $49.9 billion for Covidien, a manufacturer of minimally invasive surgical devices. More recently, in 2016, medical behemoth Abbott paid $25 billion for St. Jude Medical, a manufacturer of a multitude of medical devices.

What is important about all of these acquisitions and so many like them? They revealed a truth involving risk and capabilities that I could not see in my early years.

When I was starting my business, very green and fresh out of college, I was ready to use my time and skills within the innovation framework of my customers' organizations. I believed that the innovation processes and frameworks they were teaching us in college were the norms among manufacturing companies, and design consultants like myself were hired when their bandwidth became an issue and they had more design and development work to do than they had designers to do it.

What I discovered was that most companies did not have any designers on staff, and they did not have a defined innovation development procedure. Many were hiring consultants like myself because they knew they needed to innovate to compete, but they didn't really know what to do to innovate. They were starting projects at the wrong times, undergoing the wrong activities, and trying to get engineers to magically make design-oriented activities happen.

This revealed a truth that, as a youngster, I was shocked to learn: Large companies don't innovate, they buy innovation. They are too busy "feeding the beast" to innovate.

It would be like owning a baby elephant. You and a friend might work together—you start growing straw in a garden to feed the elephant and your friend is figuring out ways to show the elephant at circuses and petting zoos to make money. After several years, the elephant will have grown so large that all of your combined efforts are so consumed with getting enough straw into the mouth of the elephant that you have no time for anything else. In fact, you would have to recruit the help of several other friends to plant, grow, glean, bale, deliver, and feed the straw to the elephant, and therefore all the workers are content with continuing to show the elephant at the same petting zoo you have used for so many years. Innovation has stopped, because feeding the beast has consumed everything.

When corporations get large, they move slow and take a lot of effort to turn, much like a large beast or a huge ship. Maxwell Russell makes this plain in his many product-development articles for the *Harvard Business Review*. Russell often discusses that when companies start out, their means of success is innovation. You have to look no further than the companies mentioned in those mergers to see the truth of this. Medtronic started out on the innovative efforts of Earl Bakken and Walter Lillihei, who worked to put the first pacemaker into a dog and then into a human. Nostalgic photos of the garage workbench where these items were conceived reflect the innovative investigation that was going on, the heart of which is finding a creative solution to a problem.

But like most companies that grow, the business focus of Medtronic changed. Russell suggests that as a company becomes large and has investors to answer to, its focus becomes operational efficiency and profits. This all but eliminates the practices necessary for innovation. This is why he suggests that the large companies that are successful in continuing to innovate are those that create off-site, under-the-radar groups that can pursue the project in their own systematic way—and out of the view of the investors.

This is an integral concept described as *the innovator's dilemma* in Clayton Christensen's book of the same name. He acknowledges that the freedoms that are necessary for innovation can be remarkably absent in the larger and more mature corporate environment.

In the late 2000s, a Medtronic executive stated in an interview that "Medtronic does not innovate internally, we buy innovation." Now, over a decade later, we need to evaluate whether this has changed at all. For many large companies, the changing product development climate is allowing for possibilities to innovate within their borders. Scott Anthony of *Harvard Business Review*'s "Innovation" column chalks up this opportunity to pressures that startups now face; open innovation and other entrepreneurial behaviors being adopted; and new innovation startup models that rely on the strengths of large companies. (Anthony, 2021).

Whether it is these factors in the development climate or the creation of secret innovation labs hidden from corporate view, large companies are making an attempt to break free from the corporate chains that squelch innovation. Only time will tell if these efforts will be fruitful.

Holistic Thinking Isn't Just for Medicine

I felt like a ten-year-old purebred German shepherd. I was only in my mid-thirties, and my right hip felt like it had dysplasia—the kind of thing my dog had when I was a kid. There are few things that can make you feel like you are eighty years old when you are thirty-five like a bad hip. I would limp around like a war veteran with a constant pain and throbbing in my hip joint.

As most men will do, I waited until it was unbearably bad before hobbling in to see a doctor. I was prescribed some physical therapy and

Tylenol, which seemed to help a little bit, but over the years it got even worse. The pain finally compelled me to try anything that might have a shot at working, so at the advice of my wife, I went to see a holistic practitioner.

This was unusual for me, to say the least. I was not a big fan of quackery, and I often disdained those poor foolish souls who were so easily sucked into the trickery of such "traveling barbers" as chiropractors and holistic healers. When I got in to see this guy, he had the audacity to ask me all kinds of questions about my past life, as if any of that mattered for my hip. After my verbal autobiography had been delivered, he said he was going to try "pressure point therapy."

I rolled my eyes. This guy was going to poke around my body like an acupuncturist, except with his fingers instead of needles. I had better things to be doing with my time. I lay on my side, and he proceeded to push firmly with his fingers on different areas of my hip and legs, asking me if I felt pain. When he found an area that created pain, he would then begin to push on the surrounding areas, asking if I felt relief. When he found an area that provided relief, he pressed hard on that area for sixty seconds or so. He did this up and down my leg, and the entire ordeal took less than a half hour. I was quickly out the door and on my way to more important things.

When I woke up the next morning, the pain was gone. I couldn't believe it. I got up and walked around, attempting all kinds of previously painful maneuvers, but to no avail. I could not produce pain even if I tried.

I believed it was a fluke, a coincidence, or at least a placebo in my mind. After all, twelve years of constant pain could not possibly disappear from a quackery episode like I had experienced. But the pain never came back. To this day, I am pain-free from the hip problem.

My outlook on the practice of medicine changed that week. It seemed that a holistic approach meant understanding the patient as a whole, not just acutely understanding the particular predicament of the patient's pain point. With this larger body of understanding, practitioners are more fully informed, allowing them to make better decisions.

It is a bit like the old saying, "When you have a hammer, everything looks like a nail." As a health care practitioner, if the only weapons in your arsenal are drugs, surgeries or physical therapies, all of your suggestions will come from that quiver. However, fully understanding a patient's body, mind, and history of activities creates a broad starting point. Then, understanding a very broad range of possible therapies creates a large quiver with a lot of arrows. Matching the correct therapies to the multiple maladies, and eliminating the causes rather than the symptoms, is a methodology that allows the holistic practitioner to find out where creative solutions lie.

In my case, it turned out that the problem was not in my hip joint at all. It was in the ligaments that ran up and down my leg over the top of my outer hip. Repetitive activities I was involved in had caused these ligaments to become inflamed in those areas, which caused the pain. The pressure-point therapy targeted these ligaments, and a healthy dose of a different kind of physical therapy helped keep the situation from occurring again.

I realized that this kind of holistic thinking was a great problem-solving method, and not just for health issues. It's great for nearly everything, including the product design and development world that I worked in. I realized that this methodology was exactly what I had learned back in college so many years ago.

My college professor of industrial design was a temporary transplant from Germany and spoke with an endearing and often hard-to-understand German accent. The theories and methodologies he taught us often stemmed from the German "gestalt" way of thinking. Webster defines *gestalt* as "a structure, configuration, or pattern of physical, biological, or psychological phenomena so integrated as to constitute a functional unit with properties not derivable by summation of its parts." (Merriam-Webster. 2022.). The basic idea with the word is that the whole is greater than the sum of its parts, and this is where this colloquialism is derived from.

He was teaching us young, eager industrial designers that we needed to consider many things if we wanted to be effective product developers. The natural pull for designers is usually to focus on the looks, the feel, and the ergonomics of a device. Our instructor was telling us that there were so many more things we would have to pay attention to first. We had to find user needs, both small and great. We had to determine possible barriers for users, even if they were social or mental barriers.

We had to think about the financial landscape and understand the manufacturing and distribution constraints that the device would live under. We had to think of economical, ecological, and emotional issues surrounding the use of the device. We had to understand the patent landscape and the features our device must have in order to fit into that landscape. Then we had to design a device that worked in all of these areas.

This was much more difficult than an assignment that might have just asked us to come up with a creative solution for some device problem and make a prototype. In fact, trying to be creative in an environment with that many constraints seemed downright daunting.

Over the years, however, I learned that it was actually freeing to work in that kind of arena. Why? When you have been very exhaustive in identifying constraints in all these areas, you have the freedom to be creative without worrying about some hidden, lurking constraint that will come along and render your concept useless. Knowing the ropes is actually freedom to work within those ropes.

Many good ideas can get shut down early because there "might" be an issue in a certain area. For instance, creating a surgical device to be partially disposable could save money on device cost, but the idea could get shot down because people "might" not want to sterilize the reusable portion. Actually finding this out ahead of time will give you the freedom to come up with partially disposable ideas.

I walked away from my experience with that college professor understanding that if I was going to be a product designer, I had to take into account the needs of the patient, the user, the buyer, the manufacturer, the marketing folks, the business folks, the patent attorneys, the service technicians, the salespeople, and the distributors. Much as the work of a holistic practitioner became so obvious to me after my personal experience with it, this made total sense to me as well. It was obvious that if you understood all the needs in all of these areas, you could make well-informed decisions about what the end product should be, very early in the development process. In fact, you could know what it *needed* to be in order to be a successful product, just like a well-informed holistic practitioner knows what your body needs in order for a treatment to be successful.

Emotion, Experience, and Perception Are Critical

Another important thing I learned as I left the academic world of design and entered the world of commercial trade was that I was not just designing something; I was selling something as well.

I found the first question product developers must ask themselves when embarking on a product development journey, regardless of whether they are an individual entrepreneur or Proctor and Gamble, is "What am I trying to do here?" or "What am I trying to sell?" It does not matter what your particular product is. The initial answer is always the same: you are creating and selling an experience—a user experience. Successful companies know this and have capitalized on it for their success.

Emotion

Apple Computer aired a now-famous commercial during the Super Bowl in 1984 for the first Macintosh computer. This spot has gone down in history as one of the top-ten most effective television commercials of all time, and an Apple computer never appeared in the commercial at any point. Yet somehow, everyone knew what the spot was for, and it was hugely successful. The makers were very skilled in creating an experience that was comprised of emotion, perception, and the promise of satisfaction.

Good design thinking maintains that this is always exactly what is being done when a product is being developed. This is evident in the experiences that Apple users talk about compared to other personal computers, and the perception they have of themselves as being in a group that uses this product, as well as about how they are perceived by others. It is also evident in the satisfaction they feel not only with the actual computing tasks but with how they identify with, and are associated with, that product.

Apple Computer's Orwellian 1984 Macintosh Television Ad

Another good example is Caribou Coffee. Caribou has changed a fifty-cent cup of coffee into a five-dollar experience in relaxation and comfort. The feeling of a cozy cabin with a fireplace roaring and your feet up on a cozy north woods sofa is what users are getting for their five bucks.

Both of these companies created an experience for their customers in the products they've developed, and they did it intentionally and purposefully. They used three of the major elements of experience I discovered when I understood the role that the practice of design plays in the overall development process: emotion, perception, and satisfaction.

Caribou Coffee Interior Design

Experience

Let's wax technical for a moment and take emotion, something that seems ethereal, and look at the logical side of it. In order to be successful, a product must make an "emotional connection" with a user, according to Mark Dziersk, the late Vice President of Industrial Design at Brandimage and adjunct professor at Northwestern University Kellogg (Dziersk, 2010). This is a connection we cannot plan for or detect with traditional engineering methods of development. Researchers know that 95 percent of human mental processing is done on a subconscious level (Nair, n.d.). This means we must use more "human-like" methods to gain an understanding of how a product will interact with a user on that emotional level.

With this level of subconscious processing activity in continual motion, it is apparent that *all* products connect with users emotionally in some way. Unfortunately, if it is not planned, it is far more likely that the emotional connection to the user will be a negative emotion rather than a positive one.

It may be easy to envision a computer or a coffeehouse making an emotional connection with a user, but oftentimes developers and engineers have a hard time believing the need for that connection holds true when the product is something more technical, such as a medical device. With medical devices, the end user is not a typical consumer. The end user may be a physician, a nurse, a technician, or a patient. The actual customer or buyer might be a hospital purchasing person, hospital director, physician, or patient. When designing for a physician, engineers and developers may think that function stands alone as the only design criteria. However, the effect of an emotional connection can never be underestimated.

In the early 2000s, the design team at Herbst Lazar-Bell designed a line of tools for orthopedic surgery. These tools have had a positive impact on the sales of tools for the customer, Smith & Nephew, and have generated positive feedback from the surgical community. One orthopedic surgeon told researchers that "using these devices makes me feel like a rock star" after testing the prototypes. A positive user experience is important for proper device usage, as the mental state of the user plays a large role in how successful the user will be when engaging with it, and this is never more important than with medical devices. This is an example of how the use of design thinking throughout the process leads to the success of products like these.

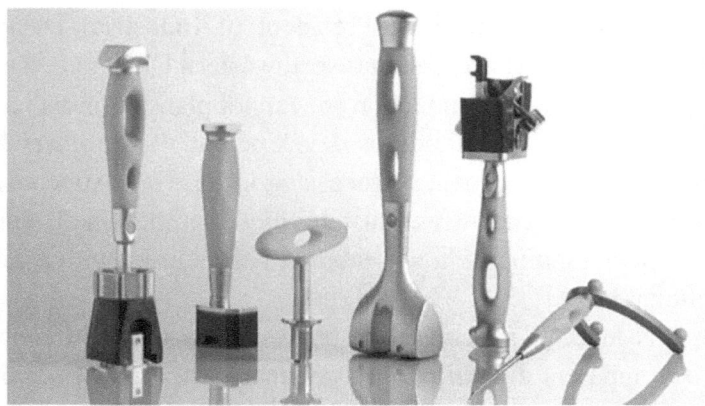

Orthopedic tools designed for Smith & Nephew by HLB

Perception

A large part of a product user's emotional connection to a product comes from perception. Human perception is an astonishing thing; however, according to visual equity analyst and principal of Applied Iconology, Inc., J. Duncan Berry, the human mind only has the ability to process 40 bps of information, yet 10,000,000 bps of visual information are thrown at it from the surrounding environment (Duncan, J. 1984). This means that people tend to only notice the things that are important to them, or things that are meaningfully different.

In experiments conducted in the UK, participants did not even notice that the experimenter was exchanged with another person when they were focused on a left-brain activity, such as looking at a map or reading a sheet of instructions. This phenomenon is called *change blindness* and is seen when a person is occupied with a mental activity. To the product designer, this means that we need to focus on what it is we want a user to perceive and devote mental attention to. This also means that the most important aspects of a product must be clear, brand recognition should be sensed, and the semantic cues of the function should be obvious to reduce the risk of hazards.

The final part of the experience and emotional connection is delivering on the promise that the product speaks. The product must be authentic in its aims and claims, and it must provide the satisfaction the user expects when it is used. It must visually and semantically speak the language of the promise that it claims to deliver, and then deliver it. Style alone will only go so far, and if there is no substance behind the style users will quickly discredit the product, which will eventually kill the brand. Beauty and brains, form and function must work together to visually deliver the emotional experience that is intended for the user. When this occurs, and satisfaction is delivered, product success is possible.

The Needs Surrounding the Need

A lot of time is spent in the academic world teaching would-be innovators to discover the "need" before designing a device to meet that need. Sounds basic, right? It is. I was completely baffled to find that anyone would do otherwise, but it was so.

Droves of people were matriculating from the academic world with engineering degrees from colleges where they'd learned to figure out how to make something work. This is a very important skill and is not meant to be minimized here in any way. However, it meant that R&D teams were being put together with engineers who were trained to figure things out, so they had to start the process with a thing. This meant that often an R&D project would start with the engineer's first idea, and then the team would begin to refine that idea in an effort to perfect it. Oftentimes this meant they did not start with the right need in mind, or with a real need at all.

To combat this way of operating in R&D, an emphasis on "needs finding" started to become popular in the late '90s and early 2000s, mostly through the work of the design school and the biodesign program at Stanford University. This was a necessary correction in innovation thinking, but I discovered that it was not where the gold is.

The gold nuggets that can transform a device from a ho-hum

modification of an existing device to something that users get excited about and embrace are actually the myriad of little needs surrounding the big need. For instance, you might have determined that the big need you are going to try to develop an innovative solution for is simplifying a long, difficult prostate surgery procedure. You did some investigation and found that the current procedure has long recovery times; is a long and therefore expensive procedure; causes a lot of pain and side effects; and does not have long-lasting results. The main need would be a cheaper, more effective, and less destructive procedure.

Knowing this is a great start, and you could begin to come up with concept ideas for a device that would accomplish some of these things. You are focused on the big need at that point. But there are also a lot of little needs surrounding that big need—little things that lend to a better ease of use, a better understanding of the proper usage scenario, safer operation procedures, and a myriad of other issues that revolve around usability and the likelihood of users adopting the device.

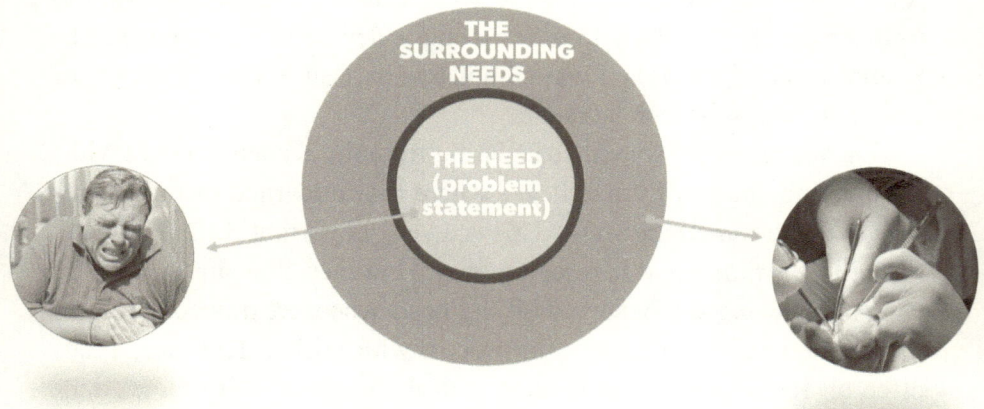

Little needs surrounding the big need lead to expanded design criteria

Over time, I discovered that these little needs can be the key to success for many innovative devices. In fact, some products completely steal market share from competitors on these little needs alone. Yet addressing these needs is often thought of as a very mysterious task, and therefore nonexistent in many product-development plans.

We will take a look at how to find and address these little needs surrounding the big need in Part Two of this book.

The Idea Man

There is a scene from the movie *Night Shift*, starring Henry Winkler and Michael Keaton, that makes me bust out into laughter every time I see it, no matter how many times I've viewed it. Michael Keaton's character fancies himself an "idea man." He walks around with a tape recorder (this was filmed in the 1980s) and speaks his ideas into it, with the intention of someday acting on his spontaneous thoughts. The problem is that none of his ideas have legs. They are not executable, and they lack the depth and substance to become real, implemented devices.

One of the things I've noticed over thirty years of product design and development is that there is no shortage of ideas. Anybody can come up with an idea, and in fact, most people do. If you were to walk through the engineering or marketing department of a manufacturer and ask each person for an idea on how the next device or system should be designed, you would get a wide variety of ideas. Everyone has ideas, and coming up with them is the easy part.

In innovation work, we can never let ourselves be fooled by the myth that every good innovation starts with an idea, and that every founder behind a company with successful innovations is an idea man, like Michael Keaton's character. This is simply not the case.

A 2019 article from the University of Virginia Department of Entrepreneurship and Innovation debunks the myth that successful innovation companies are all led by these mythical rogue leaders. (Barba-Sánchez, V. 2019). The article shares the truth that almost all such companies leverage relationships, collaboration, investment, research, and good solid development process with testing and evaluation in order to see the success they do. The lone idea man would be left with little to no success if he did not engage in these kinds of activities.

Bottom line, it is great to have creative ideas. Use them where and when it is appropriate in the development process, and you will increase your chances of innovative success.

Chapter 4

Left and Right Brain

Are We Smarter Now?

We live in a technologically fascinating age. Just like you probably have, I have seen the graphs that show the rate of technological advancement skyrocketing through history as the years go forward. But does this mean we have become smarter?

Looking just at the United States, we see generations of young Americans who can neither read nor write, nor think for themselves in any critical manner. According to a study in 2013 by the US Department of Education, 19 percent of US high school graduates can't read, and 21 percent of adults read below the fifth-grade level. (National Center for Education and Statistics, 2013).

If you remember reading about American history at all, you probably recall that one of the goals of early governments in this country was to create a strong and healthy middle class. Many people migrated to this country from homelands where a middle class was nonexistent and society consisted mostly of the extremely wealthy and the extremely poor. Migrants to America longed for the chance to not be poor, to earn a meager living, and to have a decent standard of living.

It is debatable as to whether our academic system is helping or hindering this goal. On the one hand, our students are being prepared for specialized fields of endeavor with deep study and knowledge of those areas. However, this kind of specialization may leave a vacuum of knowledge in other areas. While these students are off receiving high levels of training in their specialized area, those not pursuing higher education are living with the demonstration of a dumbed-down vocabulary in every movie, app, and video game that they watch or use. High-tech items like smartphones and video games do all the thinking and imagining for them, and they no longer have to use their brains to visualize where they are on a map and conceive an idea of how they will get from point A to point B.

I love to read the King James version of the Bible. It was compiled in 1611 AD. One of the things I love the most about it is the deeply detailed vocabulary. Thoughts and ideas are conveyed through deep, flowery descriptions, with legitimate English words that we no longer use today. Too bad. I routinely mourn the loss of good vocabulary in America as I hear new talk show hosts in their twenties and early thirties using vocabulary that seems to be ripped directly out of the 1983 movie *Valley Girl*.

I have to give a lot of credit to my tenth-grade English teacher, Mrs. DeMatties. She would give us vocabulary words and then award credit points if we came to class with examples of how we heard the words used or used them ourselves during the week. I thought it was silly and funny at the time, but now I see that she was trying to do something to stop the loss of vocabulary in America by assigning us words like *ostentatious*, *superfluous*, and *fracas*. I still use these words in my vocabulary today thanks to her.

Even though there seems to be a dumbing down occurring in our society, we have the gall to think that thousands of years ago people were much dumber than we are now. The illusion of intelligence that technology fosters has made most of modern society today arrogantly believe that our ancestors were idiots. However, we still do not know how the Egyptians made the pyramids thousands of years ago. Imagine the math those architects would have to know in order to create such a structure with no calculators and computers! The intelligence those people possessed would make today's high school graduate look like a kindergartener.

Socrates lived 2,420 years ago, Leonardo DaVinci lived 525 years ago, and Galileo lived 390 years ago. Men like this were thinking in ways that the average citizen today can't contrive in their wildest dreams. It is

31

worth noting that there was extreme ignorance and illiteracy in each of their days and ages. I think the point worth noting here is that we have struggled to create an intelligent and self-supporting middle class, and for a while it may have looked like we were succeeding, but alas, the current middle class believes they are smarter than people from 300, 500, or 2,400 years ago—yet they cannot construct a sentence with the proper vocabulary to communicate even a slight to moderate idea of complexity, leading to overused word descriptors such as *you know*, *whatever*, *right*, and *like*.

The lesson, I believe, is that we still have the same kind of brain that the Egyptians had, the same brain that Abraham had, the same brain that Adam had. There is a left side and a right side, and mankind has been utilizing the brain to a lesser or greater degree throughout all of history to respond to immediate circumstances. This, I believe, gives us hope that we can learn to harness the power and function of our own brain, even in a culture where technology seems to be replacing the need for intellect. We could then use the brain's higher function in many areas of our lives, including the area of innovation and product development.

Life Is Hard

Let's look at history. At one point, things were easier. Much easier. Our very first ancestors, Adam and Eve, lived in a perfect world where all their needs were met. I know what many of you skeptics are thinking at this point, "Adam and Eve? That's a mythical story." I won't go into details proving that the Christian Bible is the most accurate historical document on earth at this point. You can read countless books on the subject by respected scientists and professors like Lee Strobel and Greg Boyd. It's not the most supported point of view by our culture today, but then, culture has never been a good reflection of reality. It has only been a good thermometer of group thinking. Suffice it to say here that I accept the historical account of the Bible as fact, and I have never seen anything in all my research in life to contradict it.

Once evil had an introduction into this world, mankind had a much tougher existence. God said man would have to live "by the sweat of his brow." Because of this, life has been hard. For all of us. Pretty much since the beginning of time.

But humans are the only living things that were created "in the image of God." God is a thinking being with a mind, spirit, and body, and so are we. This means that we immediately begin to employ our thinking capacities to make the burden related to "the sweat of our brow" easier. Plows, fences, knives, spears, and hammers were all inventions of the human mind to make our plight easier. This continues today in the quest for innovative concepts in our product design and development efforts.

To understand how we as humans undertake this task, it is helpful to understand a little bit about how our brain works.

How Each Half of the Brain Works

The human brain is an extraordinary thing. I saw a Mercedes-Benz magazine advertisement many years ago that pictured this so well. It had an image of the human brain with the left side looking straightforward and rendered in black and white with a sentence next to it that read: "I am the left brain. I am a scientist. A mathematician. I love the familiar. I categorize. Strategic. I am practical. Always in control. A master of words and language. Realistic. I calculate equations and play with numbers. I am order. I am logic. I know exactly who I am."

The right side of the brain in this picture was colorful and flowing with form and vibrancy in an unpredictable and visually exotic fashion. It had a statement next to it that read: "I am the right brain. I am creativity. A free spirit. I am passion. Yearning. Sensuality. I am the sound of roaring laughter. I am taste. The feeling of sand beneath bare feet. I am movement. Vivid colors. I am the urge to paint on an empty canvas. I am boundless imagination. Art. Poetry. I sense. I feel. I am everything I wanted to be."

This is a nice depiction of the human brain and the differences between the left hemisphere and the right hemisphere. However, there are some stereotypes couched in this depiction that are not true, and actually inhibit innovation.

The main stereotype-busting nugget is suggested in a study done at the University of Utah examining the MRI images of 1,011 patients when engaged in certain mental activities (Study Challenges, n.d.). The results were very interesting and flew in the face of stereotypical thinking. "It is absolutely true that some brain functions occur in one or the other side of the brain. Language tends to be on the left, attention more on the right. But people don't tend to have a stronger left- or right-sided brain network. It seems to be determined more, connection by connection," the lead author of the study wrote.

He also stated, "We just don't see patterns where the whole left-brain network is more connected or the whole right-brain network is more connected in some people. It may be that personality types have nothing to do with one hemisphere being more active, stronger, or more connected."

What does this mean for us as innovators? Quite a bit, actually. What they noticed in this research, which has been corroborated with subsequent research, is that there is a certain area of the brain that fires with activity when tackling a creative problem-solving issue.

Imagine doing the work of a mechanical engineer. You have to figure out how to make things work. This means that those things have not been figured out yet. They are new. They are problems to be solved. You as the engineer are tasked with coming up with creative ways to solve these problems. You are a creative problem-solver.

If we were able to look at images of your brain when you began to conceptualize solutions to problems, we would see a certain lobe on the right side of your brain light up with activity. But whoa, wait a minute! This is the exact same lobe we saw light up when subjects were laughing at a joke! It was also the lobe that lit up when subjects were enjoying an artistic work and contemplating it. How can this be? The answer lies in the difference between linear and nonlinear thinking.

The Institute for Brain Potential teaches on a variety of brain-related topics. One of interest to me revolved around humor and creativity (King, B. 2016). In this seminar, they presented findings that showed visual representations of brain activity during the telling of a joke. The findings were quite interesting.

First, think about the anatomy of a joke. Typically, a joke starts with a buildup of linear events. Three people get on an airplane, some things happen—these are linear events, one thing logically leading to the next. Then, when the punch line is delivered, something unexpected happens. Why is it unexpected? Because it is nonlinear. It is a non sequitur. Somehow, this is funny to us. To humans, the unexpected is funny.

Think of slapstick humor. Remember how Stan Laurel and Oliver Hardy would make us laugh by unexpectedly swinging a ladder around and clobbering their counterpart in the head? We laughed because it was unexpected.

So it is with our brains. During the buildup of the joke, a lobe on the left side of the brain lights up on the visual image screen each time a linear step is revealed. When the punch line is delivered, there is a brief pause, then a lobe on the right side lights up, and the person laughs. A connection is made between the linear events of the buildup and the unexpected punch line, which ends up having an obscure, nonobvious and nonlinear connection to the sequence of events in the buildup. It takes a moment for the brain to switch to the right side and process this information, tying it to the information it received during the linear buildup.

What is the significance of all this? It is quite simple, actually. The lobe on the right side of the brain that is responsible for creative problem-solving is also the lobe that handles humor and artistic activities. The takeaway? Our brains are neuroplastic. This means they grow and morph with exercise. If we exercise our brains with artistic and humorous activities, we will be exercising the lobe responsible for creative problem-solving. As we exercise this lobe, it grows and makes us better problem-solvers, better engineers, and better designers. What a fun way to become great at what we are tasked to do!

Does this sound too good to be true? Do you want more proof? OK. Have you ever heard of desensitization therapy? This therapy is employed to combat certain phobias and other mental maladies. The essence of the therapy is that if you expose patients repeatedly to small forms of the thing they have a phobia of, they will, over time, become desensitized to the source of the phobia.

For example, if you have a fear of spiders, your therapist would start by exposing you to spider jokes and spider cartoons. Then the therapist would expose you to cute little spider stuffed animals, and finally get you to maintain your composure in the presence of an actual spider within ten feet of yourself. This kind of therapy eventually had an arachnophobe petting a live tarantula at the end of therapy.

What if you could use this type of therapy in an inverse fashion? If it works the way it was described above, could it also work to sensitize your brain to some things and neuroplastically change your brain to be predisposed to certain activities? In other words, if you exposed your brain repeatedly to humor, laughter, art, music, poetry, and design, could you exercise in advance the lobe that is responsible for not only responding to these but also creative problem-solving? Strengthen that lobe and become a better problem-solver. It is an interesting hypothesis that should someday have studies executed to prove it out.

In the absence of such studies, I will take my chances and suppose that the hypothesis is true. It's much more fun than any conceivable alternative.

Caring about People Leads to Innovation

At Kablooe Design, our mission statement is "Using innovation to improve the lives of as many people as possible with good design practices." The key point in that statement is *improving lives*. If we were just doing what we do to make money, make a better life for ourselves, or enrich our own posterity only, our mission would be void of the substantial good to society that we aim for.

If you are an innovator, this kind of thinking should lead you to think about your motivation. What is it that motivates you? Is it your ego, urging you to forge experiences that prove you are a superior designer? Is it your self and family, pressing you to make as much money as you can to create a good living for yourself and them? This is not a misguided or selfish cause. Perhaps it is your drive to create, the need to introduce creativity and innovation to the world, thus spurring mankind forward.

These are all noble causes, but none of them seems to be the supreme cause. The most supreme, selfless, and worthy cause is to help other people. This may seem altruistic, but when we examine the details,

I believe we will see that it is the only cause for innovation that has lasting value.

Let's bring this train of thought down into our world of product-development processes. Imagine you are a product-development professional assigned the task of developing a certain device for commercial production and market release. If you find yourself wanting to dive right in to prototyping and testing without spending time researching to discover user needs, what must your motivation be? Spending the time identifying user needs will only lead to designs that will make it easy and natural for users to use the device and thereby adopt it into their life and routine. This will lead to higher levels of marketplace adoption of the device and higher sales for the manufacturer.

If you want to bypass these activities for the sake of getting to a prototype quickly and testing it, you have to ask yourself if you care at all whether or not your client will be able to sell the finished product. You would even have to go a step further and ask yourself if you care whether users will get the help or improvement in their lives that the device should be promising. Is your desire to build and test greater than these larger societal needs? If so, you need to check your motives. The greater benefit of all user groups should be our prime concern as product designers. All of the other tasks in the development process should fall second to this concern.

Chapter 5

Linear vs. Divergent Thinking

Knowledge is far more than just a weird evolutionary trick invented by one of earth's species.—David Deutsch

What does it mean to be uniquely human? I defer again to the Bible. Genesis 1:26 (KJB) states that "God said, Let us make man in our image, after our likeness." (King James Bible. 2017). The fact that God can speak things into being is an amazing and mind-boggling thing in and of itself, but we will not explore that now. The salient point of that scripture for our purposes here is that humans are made in God's image and likeness. He did not say that of any other thing that He created. Thus, we have a triune being that God also possesses: a mind, body and spirit.

It is the mutual union and employment of the mind and spirit that give birth to creativity. Carried out through the body, this creativity can lead to innovation that is executable in our world, with the ability to impact the lives of others in a positive way. This is a great way to say that creativity and subsequent innovation is God-ordained.

Carry out as many experiments with dolphins and elephants as you want. No matter how many you try, you will discover that humans are uniquely the only beings that can imagine the future. No doubt, this is part of our unique nature stemming from being "made in the image of God." Imagining the future is exactly what you are doing when you are conceiving of a new idea for a device or system that potentially solves a need for someone. You are in fact imagining a future state where that need is met by something that does not yet exist in reality. This is one of the things that makes us uniquely human.

This means that we were designed to think in magnificent, colorful, and poetic nonlinear ways in addition to also thinking in the very linear and logical ways that are programmed into our psyches. What a beautiful and harmonious balance we can achieve if we engage all of the faculties that we have been designed to use.

What Have We Lost?

According to Sir Ken Robinson in his highly popular TED talk (Robinson, K. 2006) "Research has shown that young people lost their ability to think in 'divergent or non-linear ways,' a key component of creativity." This discovery was gleaned from a twenty-one-year study that followed children into adulthood, testing them for something that Mr. Robinson calls "divergent thinking." If you remember our analysis of a joke from the previous chapter, you will recall that linear thinking occurred on the left side of the brain, and nonlinear (divergent) thinking occurred on the right side of the brain. It is this kind of divergent thinking that the study refers to the loss of, which is a huge loss to creativity and potentially to innovation.

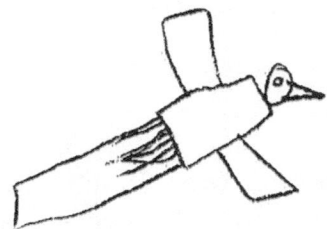

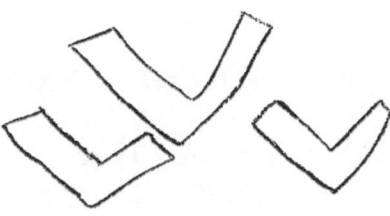

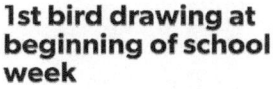

1st bird drawing at beginning of school week

2nd bird drawing at end of school week (after math workbooks)

It seems that there are many ways this breakdown of divergent thinking is fostered in our world. Mr. Robinson focuses on our educational system, which is a good place to start. But what about our commercial business world? Isn't this world an outcropping of our educational system? When we examine the evidence, it seems so.

The norm in our current business system is for large companies to hire specialists. They want people who are highly trained and extremely efficient at one particular thing. Then, by compiling enough of these people in each area of operation of their business, they can assemble and run a well-oiled machine.

I see the logic behind their thinking: the whole is exactly equal to the sum of its parts. Way to go out on a limb there, you fantastic risk-takers. In reality, the main objective of large companies is to avoid risk, which pretty much rules out all activities related to innovation. That is why they just buy innovation by acquiring other companies after the technology is proven out and the risk has been mitigated by others.

When people are hired as specialists, they often have very narrow job descriptions. This can lead to an "It's not in my job description" mentality and the inevitable situations of several groups each doing their task, then kicking the project over the wall for the next group to do their task. As you might suspect, this methodology is the complete antithesis of holistic, gestalt design thinking, yet it seems to be the norm in our commercial world today. The result is often the same as the little game known as "telephone" that we used to play when we were kids, each person whispering a message to the next, and in the end the group laughs together at how mangled the message had become.

Engineering Is Creative Problem-Solving

When you get right down to it, I think the most basic definition of engineering is "figuring out how to make things work." In essence, it is a creative problem-solving activity. All the major tasks of engineering can be reduced to various forms of problem-solving.

Remember, the lobe of the brain that is responsible for creative problem-solving is the same lobe on the right side that is engaged in artistic activities. Yet artistic endeavors are remarkably absent from most engineering training curriculums in academic America today. This is extremely unfortunate and would probably have da Vinci and Socrates rolling over in their graves. After all, Socrates wasn't teaching what he dubbed "philosophy," considering it an additional elective to an already full curriculum. No, he was teaching life. The academic philosophy that we now break down into four categories—metaphysics, epistemology, axiology, and logic—were just part of what Socrates was teaching about being a whole, thinking, and contributing member of society.

The unfortunate thing is that once people have gone through the academic system this way, they have a pretty rigid way of thinking when they get out. Rigid ways of thinking that have developed over time are hard to get rid of.

Take, for instance, the backward brain bicycle. You can find videos of this easily online. It is a fascinating experiment with a bicycle that veers to the left when you turn the handlebars to the right. The idea was to see if users could easily apply the knowledge of this steering apparatus to the rote memorization and learned motor skills they had developed over the years. The answer was a resounding *no*. Nobody could just be told about the way it worked and then morph their learned behavior instantly to accommodate the new bicycle. It took practice and learning to be able to ride it and steer predictably.

This humorous little experiment points to the truth that it is very difficult to unlearn an already learned, rigid system of understanding. Training engineers for four to six years or more with no exercising of the right side of the brain creates a person with a rigid system of operation that leaves very little room for divergent thinking and creative problem-solving.

Knowledge Does Not Equal Understanding

The point of the bicycle experiment was to show that knowledge does not equal understanding. The riders of the bicycle were given complete knowledge of the operation of the bicycle before they hopped on and attempted to ride. Yet they did not possess enough understanding of the correct operational procedures to navigate the vehicle correctly. It makes sense then to conclude that knowledge and understanding are not the same thing.

It seems that in order to solve a problem, you must possess a certain amount of understanding about that problem. Understanding the user, the user's needs, and the circumstances and environment around that problem all lead to a full understanding of the problem. Once that level of understanding is achieved, creative solutions will begin to flow.

All the knowledge in the world about the turn radius of the bike, the movement of the wheel in relation to the handlebars, the forces of inertia, and the knowledge of the center of gravity had no effect on the successful performance of the driver. Only when the driver possessed an understanding of the feeling of the bike moving in his hands and under his body did he have the tools he needed to construct a method of steering that worked for both him and the bicycle.

Ethnographers over the years have talked about the goal of achieving *emic validity* for the subjects they were studying. This validity was nothing more than a deep understanding of the situation from the user's point of view. The goal was understanding—much like the goal of the product designer and innovator of today is to empathize with users and understand the world from their point of view.

Where Does Innovation Live?

Art Fry was the inventor of the Post-it Note. He gives a nice lecture titled "The Post-it Note Was Not an Accident" (Fry, A. 2009). It is a very worthwhile lecture if you ever get a chance to listen to him give it. One of his major points in the talk is that freedom leads to innovation.

Art was working at 3M when he invented the Post-it Note. He talks at length about the freedom the company gave him and his team to innovate, creating an environment that was suitable to creativity with its culture, systems, and accoutrements. This paved the way for him to come up with an idea for a bookmark that could be used in the hymnbooks for his church choir. These bookmarks eventually gained purpose for use and became the Post-it Note.

Innovation lives where there is freedom to innovate. The industrial revolution in America was partially fueled by the fact that most people were free to do what they wanted, and with the need to make our burdens lighter, necessity always becomes the mother of invention. Great innovations began to pop up that made farming and manufacturing more efficient and cost-effective. I don't need to point out many more items than the assembly line, the automobile, and the cotton gin to prove this point. Thus, creating an environment and culture for designers and engineers to work within that fosters freedom and creativity is a critical element to successful innovation and cannot be overlooked.

Ken Robinson pointed out that divergent thinking is a key component to creativity. Divergent thinking does not follow a sequential linear pattern. Unlike linear thinking, divergent thinking can seem to make no sense at all to the thinker, or to outside observers. Divergent thinking leaves the linear sequence of logic and branches off into rabbit trails in all directions, considering the unlikely and unassociated what-ifs that wander away from the linear train of thought.

Using divergent thinking can cause you to look for and discover relationships with seemingly unrelated things. If you were in a class discussion where the instructor is explaining to your groups the steps to creating a wooden coffee table; and you had heard about cutting and shaping the wood, putting it together, sanding it smooth; and just as your instructor begins to tell you about staining the wood you get an idea and ask the question, "What if we poured concrete and feathers all over the top of it first?" you would be using divergent thinking. Your brain left the logical, sequential path of the storyline and began to wander, thinking about unrelated things: *Birds ... aren't they pretty? We want our coffee table to be pretty ... what about feathers? Sanded wood is smooth. Concrete is rough, but sturdy. We want our coffee table to be sturdy. Could we use concrete, and could we make it become smooth?* This is divergent thinking, and you can see why it is regarded as a key component of creativity. Without it, the development of new thoughts would have to take a much longer and more straightforward path.

Our brains were designed to ask questions and present us with what-if situations. I want to be clear here in letting you know that I am no expert in the brain and its activities. I am not a scientist with a background of study in brain activity. I have one, though, and I have read many articles and papers on the subject. When I talk of these matters in this book, I am only reflecting on some of the most interesting things I have read about from other people's research.

A Harvard study from 2018 (Beaty, Roger E., et al. 2018) used MRI imaging to reinforce what a University of Utah study discovered. In the

Utah study, researchers concluded that personality type had nothing to do with having a "stronger" left or right hemisphere. In the Harvard study, researchers concluded that creativity didn't so much come from one particular region of the brain but more from various regions being able to connect and communicate strongly and efficiently.

"It's the synchrony between these systems that seems to be important for creativity," said Roger Beaty, the first author on the study. "People who think more flexibly and come up with more creative ideas are better able to engage these networks that don't typically work together and bring these systems online."

These were brain regions that would normally not work in harmony with each other. If we look at our divergent-thinking example, however, it makes perfect sense. We are taking linear inputs and quickly switching to a fuzzier, cloud way of thinking, then moving back to linear to put the pieces together. This is how we understand that at the heart of creativity is the ability to look at seemingly unrelated things and make connections with them. Strong connections between different neural networks allows us to do this.

How Were Our Brains Made?

The results of the Harvard study found that three distinct brain networks were key to the most creative thinking. These are known as the *default network* (related to brainstorming and daydreaming), *executive control network* (which activates when a person needs to focus), and *salience network* (known for detecting environmental stimuli and switching between executive and default brain networks).

This layout of our brain networks and functions seems to be the perfect example of the whole being more than the sum of its parts. When each of these neural networks is working on its own, it is completing the work it was designed for, such as focused activities, response to stimuli, and daydreaming. But when they are pulled together and used as a closely communicating neural network group, the functional output is creativity. I would even propose that the output is *functional* creativity, which is important for innovation because you must remember that innovation only exists if it can be applied in the real world. One could argue that the daydreaming output of the default network alone is creativity, but it is likely not functional creativity until it is connected with the activity of the other networks.

In this case, we see that creativity is the output of several discrete brain functions working together, showing us that the whole truly is greater than the sum of its parts. Socrates was onto something, even without our MRI data. Thank goodness we have that data today and can see visual proof.

The Mayo Clinic tells us that our brain's hemispheres are divided into four lobes. (Mayo Clinic Foundation, 2016)

1. The *frontal lobes* control thinking, planning, organizing, problem-solving, short-term memory, and movement.
2. The *parietal lobes* interpret sensory information, such as taste, temperature, and touch.
3. The *occipital lobes* process images from your eyes and link that information with images stored in memory.
4. The *temporal lobes* process information from your senses of smell, taste, and sound. They also play a role in memory storage.

We also know that the *cerebellum*, which is a wrinkled ball of tissue below and behind the rest of our brain, works to combine sensory information from the eyes, ears, and muscles to help coordinate movement. Right below this is the *brainstem*, which links the brain to the spinal cord. It controls many functions vital to life, such as heart rate, blood pressure, and breathing. This area is also important for sleep.

In almost predictable fashion, we see that the *deep* things, like deep thoughts and emotions, come from sections deep inside the center of the brain. These structures control emotions and memories. Known as the *limbic system*, they come in pairs, with each part of the system duplicated in the opposite half of the brain. The *thalamus* acts as a gatekeeper for messages passed between the spinal cord and the cerebral hemispheres. The *hypothalamus* controls emotions. It also regulates your body's temperature and controls crucial urges, such as eating or sleeping. Lastly, the *hippocampus* sends memories to be stored in appropriate sections of the cerebrum and then recalls them when necessary.

American social psychologist Barbara Fredrickson found that if we choose to think of more events as positive rather than neutral, and experience positive emotions like appreciation and joy, we experience an upward spiral of emotion, which improves and increases our radius of awareness. Fredrickson calls this the Broaden-and-Build theory (Fredrickson, B. L. 2001). She conducted randomized control studies and found that positive emotions change our view and even our peripheral vision. They open us and change our outlook on the environment and the way we approach tasks. This applies to creativity and helps explain the results of the Harvard study.

Fredrickson posits that as our view of the world expands (from positive emotions), we become more flexible, innovative, and creative, and we are able to see solutions we would not normally see (Fredrickson, 2003). Compare this to the Harvard study, which shows that using different networks of the brain together and increasing their ability to connect leads to creativity. Thus, Fredrickson's conclusion is that cultivating positive emotions is a great way to increase our creative output. This is why tools such as a gratitude journal can be effective for well-being and for creativity as well.

So were we designed to think this way? If we look at instructions from the designer of our brains, we see that we are expected to be joyful (Psalm 5:11), thankful (1 Thes. 5:18), peaceful (Rom. 12:18), and to rejoice (Psalm 35:9). It sounds like the designer of our brains knew from the beginning what we have discovered in this century. And if He expects us to be creative beings, which He does, then He knows that these instructions are good for delivering creativity.

The Creator Always Knows More than the "Create-ee"

It seems that God knows what is good for us. After all, centuries before we understood germs, bacteria, and the transmission of disease, He gave instructions for washing and carcass disposal. He also told us about the currents of the oceans and the cycle of rain and clouds long before we defined ocean currents or the water cycle. Just as He let Adam use his creativity with the job of classifying the animal species, so He has empowered us to use our brains creatively, and to use them to innovate.

Chapter 6

Humor and Creativity

What's So Funny about Innovation?

For most of its history, Kablooe Design did not have an intentional marketing plan. Word-of-mouth referrals brought in most of our business. As we began to develop a culture and personality for the company, we began to see the things that were important to us, and I began to understand the importance of making sure those things were communicated to our potential customers. This was the birth of any marketing-related thinking within the company.

One of the things that was of high importance to myself and many others in the company was the ability to have fun at work. I had often said that if you couldn't have fun at the place you go every day and spend a majority of your time, what's the point? We all liked to have fun, and we made the workplace a place where that could happen. We had basketball hoops and ongoing tournaments, as well as dart, foosball, ping-pong, and fantasy foosball tournaments. But aside from these structured events, having a good time using wit and humor in our everyday dealings with each other laid a foundation of fun in our days, and reflected the fact that we loved the work we did.

As time went on, I believed this element of fun in the workplace was more important than just goofing around and having a good time. There was something about it that made me believe it was more important than that. As I reflected on reasons why this might be true, I was reminded how the neurotransmitter dopamine works in the brain. During an experience that is enjoyable, such as humor and fun (things that make us laugh and smile), dopamine is released in the brain and creates a pleasurable feeling. That leaves an impression on our memory cells, and later, when those memories are brought to the surface of our thinking, our brain releases dopamine again, and we get that same good feeling again.

It dawned on me that this was the greatest and most true-to-our-nature form of marketing that Kablooe could do. I called it dopamine marketing. Dopamine marketing was simply making sure that when our potential customers interfaced with us on any level, they always felt an element of fun. This would release dopamine in their brains, and the next time Kablooe was brought to mind, dopamine would release again, and they would have a good feeling about us.

People tend to make buying decisions based in large part on emotions, so having a good feeling about our company, even if it was from dopamine, would increase the chance that they would trust us and choose to use our company. I should have kept track of statistics and wrote a paper on the subject. It would have been a curious study.

The Good Humor Man Is Smarter Than You Think

In the previous chapter, we discussed nonlinear (divergent) thinking, and how the left and right sides of the brain work in relation to art and humor. We talked about the anatomy of a joke, and the linear sequence of events leading up to a nonobvious event that the listener has to try to make sense of in the punch line. What makes a joke a good one is the a priori knowledge that will most likely be thought of by listeners as the tie between the two, and then using it to bring listeners to a realization that they would not have reached otherwise.

I think it benefits us here to take a closer look at humor to see why this is important for innovators. First, when your brain experiences humor and laughter, it creates increased levels of BDNF (King, B. 2016). BDNF, short for brain-derived neural factor, is a protein that is partly responsible for the neuroplasticity of the brain and the storage of information (memory). So how important is it? Studies have shown that 95 percent of all brain activity is habit. This means that 95 percent of everything your brain is doing is being drawn from old stored information, and BDNF is responsible for storing it.

Because our brain is neuroplastic, it changes with activity. BDNF is also responsible for this neuroplasticity, which allows a part of the brain to grow with usage. Remember, if we continually use that lobe on the right while doing artistic or humorous activities, we exercise it, much like a muscle in a weight lifting routine. So humor not only exercises that part of the brain, it also helps provide the chemical that allows it to change and strengthen. Since this is the lobe that also drives our creative problem-solving engine, it gives us a stronger creative problem-solving muscle and makes us better design engineers.

Play and Creativity

There has been a fair amount of research done that supports these ideas. One recent study showed a strong correlation between humor, wit, improvisational comedy training, and a better ideation outcome, in both quantity and quality (Kudrowitz 2010). In the study, subjects who produced the highest quantity of potential solutions to a problem were also those who had the most prolific results in wit exercises and had training in improvisational comedy.

Comedy training is a great example to support our claims of the humor/innovation connection described earlier. This training would have helped these subjects ideate better for two main reasons. First, it helped them learn skills that were nearly identical to the skills needed for ideation work. Ideating to find new ideas and solutions involves looking at seemingly unrelated things and finding connections. This is precisely what improvisational comedy training exercises focus on. Second, they were repeating these exercises over and over, which changed and improved that lobe on the right with the neuroplastic regeneration that comes from repeated use. They worked out this lobe like a muscle gets worked out in a gym and grew its capacity to perform.

Anne Marie Thomas, in her book *Making Makers* (Thomas, A. P. 2014.), talks about the need to let kids have fun by doing things with their hands so that they learn skills that will enable them to build things. Her thesis revolves around the idea that kids will never grow to make things and innovate if they don't learn to love the hands-on skills needed to do it. But it seems that one of the keys here is the "having fun" part. If children truly have fun while learning to build with their hands, all of the dopamine and right-brain exercising will be at their disposal to help them use those skills to creatively solve problems and be future innovators.

God gave us a sense of humor. It stands to reason that a created thing cannot have anything in and of itself that the creator of that thing does not have. If I were to make a clay pot on a spinning wheel, the only reason I could achieve a reasonably round shape for it is because I can conceive in my mind what roundness is. With that knowledge of roundness, I can impart the essence of it through my hands and into the pot I am making.

The only reason we possess a sense of humor is because our creator embodies the qualities of humor in His omniscient presence, and in creation he bestows some of those traits to us. I have found that He usually has a good reason for doing things—sometimes many good reasons, but they aren't apparent to us at the start and sometimes never are. Perhaps one good reason He gave us the ability to create and partake in humor was to exercise our brains so we can be problem-solvers. After all, survival is all about problem-solving. If this hypothesis is true, He also made us creative and made us to be problem solvers. Is there precedent for this assumption? Let's take a look at history.

Turn the clock all the way back to before 4000 BC. God creates Adam, and instead of leaving him standing around twiddling his thumbs, He gives him a job. Most people don't take the time to discover that Adam had a real job. God told him to look at all the created things and give them names—classify them. Today we call this taxonomy, and it is a biology term that refers to the branch of science concerned with classification, especially of organisms.

Today when scientists investigate and classify living things, they have a lot of predecessors to look to for wisdom in forming their conclusions. Imagine being the first guy to do this. It wouldn't be so easy without something in your memory to look back to for comparison. Talk about creative problem-solving! This new scientist role took a ton of raw problem-solving capability on Adam's part, and no doubt his sense of humor was active at the time too. After all, without humor, who would have named an elephant *Phil*? In Hebrew, this is the word for elephant. Did Adam speak Hebrew? We may never know, but I can sure imagine some chuckling going on as he was classifying and naming hedgehogs, geckos, and bombardier beetles.

Fast forward several hundred years to Noah having to build a gigantic sea vessel when his occupation was being a preacher, or a thousand years further to when Nehemiah had to supervise the rebuilding of the city of Jerusalem. Creative problem-solving examples are found everywhere throughout history, but the point of these examples is that they were people with very specific and incredibly difficult missions from God, and He equipped them with the mental capacities to do the job.

And let's not forget that God shows us some pretty clear examples of His own sense of humor in recorded scripture. In 1 Samuel, chapter 5 (KJV), we read:

> After the Philistines had captured the ark of God, they took it from Ebenezer to Ashdod, and brought it into the temple of Dagon and placed it next to this statue. When the people of Ashdod got up early the next morning, there was Dagon, fallen with his face to the ground before the ark of the Lord. So they took Dagon and returned him to his place. But when they got up early the next morning, there was Dagon, fallen with his face to the ground before the ark of the Lord. This time, Dagon's head and both of his hands were broken off and lying on the threshold. Only Dagon's torso remained." (King James Bible, 2017.)

It's not hard to see God chuckling a little bit as he watched these folks come into their temple each morning to see the statue of their idol fallen on its face, as if it were worshiping the ark of God. If I were doing this to their statue, I would probably be chuckling a bit too.

God has a sense of humor. He uses it, and He gives it to us. There are more reasons than we can know why He did this, but our discoveries about how humor positively affects our brains gives us some clues into God's ultimate wisdom.

We were designed as wonderful, amazing beings, with capabilities and internal operations that are amazing and downright unexplainable. I remember being in the sixth grade and learning several theories of how humans came into being described to the class. I remember when the theory of evolution was explained, and even as a ten-year-old child, I thought, "Wait a minute, that makes no sense." Even a ten-year-old can spot the impossibilities of the theory. Monkeys changing into humans … it sounded like a bad movie plot.

Even at that young age, I knew what the scientific method was because it had just been taught to us in science class. It was also obvious that no one had ever observed a monkey change into a human and leap from one species to the next. Fortunately, the teacher just introduced macroevolution as a theory, and I was content to let it go at that.

Later, in tenth-grade social studies, the subject was introduced again, in more detail. Yet it still was taught to us as a theory among other theories, and an unproven one at that. Somewhere in the decades since, it has become the most commonly accepted theory on the origin of life, at least in the United States. I am not sure how or why this happened over the years, but when I hear people talking about it, I want to pull out and play my "Emperor's New Clothes" card.

If you recall, in the story of "The Emperor's New Clothes," all of society gets swept along into thinking that the emperor has new clothes, but the clothes are invisible to fools. Nobody wants to be a fool, so they all agree with each other that the clothes look beautiful, even when there are absolutely no visual facts to support their thinking. This goes on until a child comes along and, in the usual manner of children, shouts out that the emperor has no clothes, and the entire lie is revealed.

Evolution? From monkeys? One species changing into another? It has never been seen. Microevolution, sure … things that are designed to undergo change based on a myriad of factors. But one species completely changing into another has never been seen. Let me know when it is. Until then, I call an "Emperor's New Clothes" on the whole ordeal.

I remember working on a project that required our team to develop concepts for a device that would be used to treat a malady within the human eye. Our work on the project required a bit of research on our part, as it often does, to become familiar with the eye. I remember being fascinated by the complex abilities and functions of the eye. I was awestruck that all of those tiny, intricate components and functions could all work together symbiotically to make a functioning eye.

I began to wonder how any organism could have evolved over long periods of time that needed the eye. Either the entire eye, with all of its intricate and codependent functions and parts, would have had to come into being at one time in one animal, or it would have had to evolve part by part, function by function, over a long period of time, and never function or work as an eye for all that time, leaving the poor animal to walk around blind, and plunging to its death at every cliff.

The first instance is just silly, and the second is impossible. And that was just the eye. I was soon thereafter engaged on an ear project. Talk about complex ... don't get me started.

So this leaves us with the knowledge that we were meticulously and skillfully designed as very complex beings to operate in very complex and wonderful ways. This includes our innate ability to enjoy humor, and thereby grow our brains to solve creative problems.

Chapter 7

Brain Building

What Do We Pay Attention To?

Our brains are designed to notice what is different

When you looked at the picture of the penguins, what was the first thing you focused on? It was the white outlined penguin, wasn't it? It stands to reason that if most of what our brain is doing at any moment is stored information, it will seem like the same old, same old to the brain. Everything will take on a nominal value. Then the things that are different will stand out, and your brain will take notice. The pink penguin is easily spotted among the sea of black and white ones.

This trait can be understood to be very helpful in most situations. Think of driving in heavy traffic. Automobiles are everywhere, but when a person on a bicycle enters the lane next to you, you become keenly aware of his presence. He is different than the rest of the vehicles around you and garners a higher level of attention from your brain. This is a handy safety mechanism for us.

Visual perception is an interesting trait and is different from visual acuity. Visual acuity is all about how well your body's visual system handles light when it enters. Visual perception is all about what our brains understand from that light entering the visual system. According to the Interaction Design Foundation (2017):

> The visual perception of colors, patterns, and structures has been of particular interest in relation to graphical user interfaces (GUIs) because these are perceived *exclusively* through vision. An understanding of visual perception therefore enables designers to create more effective user interfaces."

Physiologically, visual perception happens when the eye focuses light on the *retina*. Within the retina, there is a layer of photoreceptor (light-receiving) cells that are designed to change light into a series of *electrochemical signals* to be transmitted to the brain. Visual perception occurs in the brain's *cerebral cortex*; the electrochemical signals get there by traveling through the optic nerve and the thalamus. (Wikipedia, 2022.) The process can take a mere 13 milliseconds.

Different attributes of visual perception are widely used in GUI design. Many designers apply gestalt principles (i.e., how humans structure visual stimuli) to the design of GUIs so as to create interfaces that are easy for users to perceive and understand. The visual perception of affordances (action possibilities in the environment) is another example of how the understanding of visual perception is a critical item in any designer's tool kit.

The importance of this isn't only for the design of information on electronic displays but for devices and other objects as well. The idea of affordances is extremely important with medical devices and other task-critical items where the safety of users and others could be at risk if misuse occurs. The idea is that several action options could exist that might be employed by the user for an interactive task with the device, and the best use of affordance by the device's designer is to make the brain's decision to choose the correct, safest, and most effective options made clear by all of the visual cues the device offers.

There have been instances where clinical personnel were using feeding tubes on patients, but the connections and valves looked very similar to vascular tube systems, and the tubes were hooked up to the wrong system, resulting in patient death. Unfortunate instances like these demonstrate the importance of the intentional look, feel, and understanding of a device or system. With medical devices, lives are on the line, and these types of design considerations are extremely important.

Semantics

This is why semantics are so important in innovative product development and design. Wikipedia defines semantics this way:

> **Semantics** (from Ancient Greek: σημαντικός *sēmantikós*, "significant") is the linguistic and philosophical study of meaning in language, programming languages, formal logics, and semiotics. It is concerned with the relationship between *signifiers*—like words, phrases, signs, and symbols—and what they stand for in reality, their denotation. Gestalt principles of things like similarity, continuation, and proximity. (Wikipedia, 2022.)

As device designers, we have to understand that everything visual about our potential innovation is a signifier. With this understanding, we can begin to appreciate why the aesthetics, ergonomics, and visual design language of a device or system are so important. They are more than just a fun look to something. They actually foster safety and efficacy if we pay attention to them and understand them correctly.

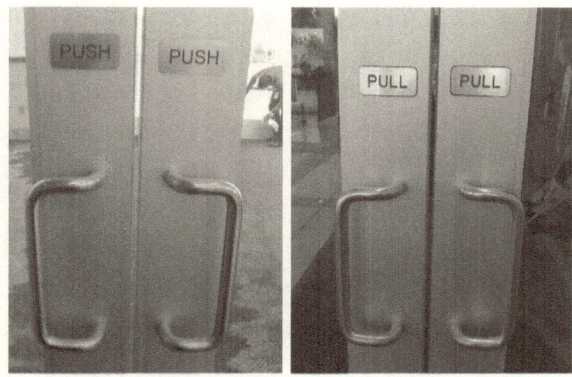

Semantics deal with visual signifiers that convey meaning

A good example is the door handle shown in the photo. We can see the affordance issues that result from the structure of the visual stimuli. Visually, there is nothing to distinguish the handle from one side of the door from the handle on the other side. Yet they have exactly opposite functions. Consequently, users are frequently frustrated with this device by initiating the opposite action necessary to achieve the desired function.

Understanding how the brain takes visual cues, latches onto patterns, and recognizes continuations and similarities would help a designer construct a door handle that would have less error. With critical devices, less error means less risk and less harm. The door handle in the second picture is semantically easier to understand and therefore encounters less user error.

The takeaway from these studies is that even though our brain is designed to naturally notice those things that are different and stand out, it is doing it from a sense of homeostasis. Your brain, just like the rest of your body, wants to create a level of homeostasis. Your body has a constant drive to maintain overall homeostasis, which means that there are prescribed levels of substances and actions in the body that are optimum for its survival, and it strives to keep those levels.

One simple example is perspiration. As your body begins to detect that its temperature level is higher than it should be, it sends saline to the outer surface of your skin where it can evaporate and create a cooling effect. You don't make this happen consciously; your body does it automatically because it was designed to do so.

To understand how deeply focused your body is on doing this, consider something as deeply internal as calcium levels. You may lack an appropriate amount of calcium in your diet, but when you get your blood test taken, it shows normal levels of calcium. Why is this? In your body's quest for homeostasis, it detects the lack of calcium and begins pulling it from your bones to create the proper level. It shows to be fine in your bloodstream, but you are sacrificing the health of your bones by forcing your body to draw precious calcium away from them. Osteoporosis is then on your doorstep.

So when your brain notices the odd or different thing, it is doing so because it intuitively wants to take those anomalies and reduce them to things that have closure, symmetry, and a possibility of being well understood. If your brain can't find the visual stimuli to do this, it has to make something up, introducing an element of chance into the activity and increasing the likelihood of error and harm.

Perception Blindness

Earlier in the book we talked about the phenomenon of the human brain known as *perception blindness* or *change blindness.* You recall that this phenomenon is observed when a visual change is introduced into a person's visually active field but the person's brain creates no mental awareness of the change, leaving the person completely unaware that the change has occurred. This can seem very funny at times and has led to humorous, nonscientific, video-clip studies on such mediums as Spike TV as we discussed earlier. But scientific studies have been done as well.

The setup is to bring subjects into a situation where they will be given a short task. In one situation, the task could be filling out a short application form with a pencil and paper. In another, it could be looking at a map in order to give another person traveling directions. During this task, a major change to the subject's environment is introduced. The person giving the paper form and instructions, or the person asking for directions on the map, quickly ducks out of sight behind some object, and a different person appears in their place. In roughly 70 percent of situations, the subject did not notice that the other person had changed.

The explanation behind this phenomenon is quite simple. The human eye is hit with about 10 million bits of visual information every second. The brain, however, only has the capacity to process 40 bits per second. This is a huge gap. Therefore, the brain only chooses to process the things that are deemed most important at the time. When the brain is given a task to do, the visual information related to that task is accepted by the brain, and other stimuli are discarded.

It may seem like perception blindness completely contradicts the earlier discussed phenomenon of the brain noticing things that are different, as with perception blindness the brain *doesn't* notice the thing that is different. Even though these may seem contradictory, one could argue that the brain is really striving for the same thing in both situations.

When the brain is trying to make sense out of a map, it is striving for closure, proximity, and similarity, all of which are gestalt principles of perception, just like when it was noticing something different and striving to file that thing in an orderly way to create mental homeostasis. Becoming so engrossed in the task of the map work that it cannot devote attention to its surroundings is not a lack of the presence of the noticing function, but rather a lack of bandwidth for that function. The bandwidth for the function remains the same in both situations; it is just applied in each by priority.

Both of these phenomena help us as creators of innovation by giving us a bit of insight into how the brains of our users may operate. By understanding the limited capabilities of our users' perception, and the tendencies their brains have for organizing and understanding visual cues, we can be a little smarter about how our devices will look, feel, and operate in regard to the users' interaction with it, making our designs safer and more accepted by the users we are attempting to improve the lives of.

Murphy's Law

Most of us remember something called Murphy's Law, which is a sarcastic take on how things turn out. The phony but humorous so-called law states that if something can go wrong, it will, and it will do so at the worst possible time.

Even though this is far from a scientific law, it bears some importance on what we do as creators of devices and systems. Because we are often creating things for a large number of users, we have to remember that the likelihood of hazardous situations with our innovations will increase as the user population does. Thus, as developers, we take on the mind-set that if people can use our device incorrectly, they will. We then task ourselves with figuring out how we can design the device so it *can't* be used incorrectly.

This is what the entire risk-management part of our development projects is all about. In the medical-device world, we are required to have something called a *quality management system* (QMS) that governs our development process. One aspect of this system is a required risk-management plan. In the risk-management plan, we identify potential risks, hazards, and harms and rate them according to their likelihood and severity. We then list ways to mitigate these risks, with solutions coming from three categories in order of preference.

The first mitigation category is a change to the design of the device or system that lowers the chance of the hazard to an acceptable level. The second is adding an element to the design or system that potentially diverts the hazard or protects the user from the hazard. The last resort is to give the user some kind of written instruction on a label or in an instructional document that explains how to avoid the risk of the potential hazard.

As designers, we have to understand that if we leave options open for users to misunderstand and then misuse a device, a percentage of them will. Based on what we know about perceptive abilities, and the fact that users will not necessarily be focused on everything they need to do to operate the device correctly, but rather what is important to them at the moment, we must make sure that these occurrences have been taken into account and the risk reduced to acceptable levels in our designs.

The Whole Is More Than the Sum of Its Parts

How do we build our brains and increase our innovative capacities so we can imagine creative ways to capture our future users attention appropriately and reduce misuse risk? We have already seen some ways to do this individually: exercise the right side of your brain with humor, art, poetry, music, comedy, comics, wit, and plain old good-time laughter. We could add to these a couple of helpful things.

Think Positively

Positive thinking can lead to increased resilience, which helps build coping skills that lead to better problem-solving skills (Association for Psychological Science – APS. n.d.). And remember, innovation is all about creative problem-solving. Resilience actually refers to our ability to cope with problems in general, but that ability in our brains also transfers to creative development problems. Resilient people are able to face a crisis or trauma with strength and resolve, and believe me, sometimes the responsibility of having to solve a creative problem by developing an innovative device feels like a crisis or trauma. Rather than falling apart in the face of such stress, resilient people have the ability to carry on and eventually overcome adversity, a much-needed skill for the innovator.

It's not surprising to see that positive thinking can play a major role in resilience. When dealing with a challenge, optimists typically look at what they can do to fix the problem. Instead of giving up hope, they marshal their resources and are willing to ask others for help, both necessary modes of action for innovation (Fredrickson, B. L. 1998).

Researchers have also found that in the wake of a crisis, such as a terrorist attack or natural disaster, positive thoughts and emotions encourage thriving and provide a buffer against depression among resilient people (Fredrickson et al., 2003). Fortunately, experts also believe that such positivism and resilience can be cultivated. By nurturing positive emotions, even in the face of terrible events, people can reap both short-term and long-term rewards, including managing stress levels, lessening depression, and building coping skills that will serve them well in future development and innovation challenges as they exercise that part of the right side of the brain that is used for creative problem-solving.

Help Others

A 2017 study out of Columbia University and MIT investigating the effects of helping other people (Doré et al., 2017) and a 2005 study in the International Journal of Behavioral Medicine (Post, S. G. 2005). both show that because heightened levels of self-focused attention are common in depression, the more people help others, the more their helping behavior predicted a reduction in their own depression, thanks to the use of reappraisal in their own daily lives. Reappraisal is the ability to look at your situation from a different point of view—an important ability for someone tasked with creative thinking and innovating. Follow-up analysis of the studies further showed that this increase in reappraisal in people's lives also affected their mood and subjective happiness, which we have seen increases BDNF and exercises the right side of the brain.

Interestingly, messages that used other-focused language (e.g., second-person pronouns such as *you* and *your*) were considered more helpful and garnered more gratitude from participants. In fact, using other-focused language not only helped the people in need but also those who were helping. This finding suggests that providing emotional support to others and empathizing with them can increase reappraisal and lead to better psychological outcomes for those who are providing the support. Thus, helping others helps you to build the creative problem-solving part of your brain.

Trust Your Creator

Let's face it: when you have honest-to-goodness trust in someone or something, that leads to a confidence that is very difficult to shake. Think of gravity. You probably have a lot of trust in the effects of gravity always being there for you, bringing you back to the ground after you jump up. This in turn probably gives you great confidence that you are not going to just float off into space at some random time, and that confidence is the opposite of fear. This is important from a creative problem-solving perspective because fear has a way of locking up our brains and stifling creative thinking. Confidence eliminates fear and frees the brain to engage in deep creative thought.

This benefit grows even bigger and stronger when the trust is applied to our Creator. Remember the Creator/createe discussion? If we trust that our Creator can give us everything we need to succeed at the task set in front of us, it gives us great confidence and eliminates the fear that we won't succeed, which in turn helps facilitate the results we are looking for. Sort of a self-fulfilling prophecy, but with an actual connection to the source of all the energy in our universe.

Trusting your Creator is the first step to developing a relationship with Him that will yield eternal benefits, but that is the subject of another book at another time. Suffice it to say here that this kind of relationship with and trust of your Creator will yield benefits when it comes to using your brain in a clear and effective way—truly a good thing for innovators!

Eat Right

Oh boy. Volumes have been written on studies of nutrition and how our bodies and minds are affected. One section of one chapter in a book about creative design and innovation is not going to do this topic justice, but I can just hit a few high points here that make a difference.

First, I believe I am uniquely qualified to comment on this issue because my wife is a holistic health practitioner and my personal "doctor," so I hear this stuff from her day in and day out. Things we put into and onto our bodies I often hear from her are the "biggest offenders" in destroying our health. Why? Toxins.

Toxins in your body can cause damage to your blood–brain barrier, and this in turn can cause brain fog and other impediments to proper brain function. Where does the buildup of toxins in the body come from? Many places, including our environment and pollution, but the biggest source of toxins is the things you put in your mouth.

Think about it—so much of our diet today is not really food but an assortment of chemicals shoved into something that resembles the shell of a food product. Your body was not designed to ingest and deal with these kinds of chemicals. Your body was designed to intake raw plants and grains and other very natural food items. What does your body do with all that extra chemical stuff that it was not designed to deal with? Don't know? Neither does your body, so it stashes the junk away in various places, which leads to maladies of all kinds.

One of them can be the deterioration of the blood–brain barrier. According to information from the *Journal of Neurology, Neurosurgery, and Psychiatry,* "The mature nervous system is remarkably vulnerable to toxin induced damage ... to affect gait and posture, the special senses, behavior and cognition, and produce a complex pattern of clinical signs and symptoms" (Harris, 2004). This depletion of cognition could obviously be a barrier to the clear, concise creative thinking that is so necessary for creative problem-solvers. Good cognition is the opposite of brain fog, which would impede creative thought.

528hz and 417hz Solfeggio Tones

Scientists have discovered that everything in this universe vibrates at a frequency. This not only includes your body but also the trillions of molecules that construct the matter around us. According to the folks at TO112, "The 528 Hz Solfeggio Frequency is thought to resonate at the core of everything; connecting our heart, our spiritual nature, and the divine harmony." (TO112 Expert, 2020)

The train of thought here is that the 528 Hz frequency is a musical tone that has been used since ancient civilizations for positive things. Think about how often we generally use music to help change our mood. If we are stressed, we naturally put on some slow, calming music to ease our minds. Sometimes when our mood is dragging, we listen to upbeat music to help pump up our energy for the day. It is said that music has a profound effect on our being, even at a cellular level.

The 528 Solfeggio Frequency seems to have a deep-rooted relationship with nature and appears in many songs, most famously John Lennon's "Imagine," which was composed in this frequency. It is said to increase clarity of mind and awareness, activate creativity, and also activate your imagination, intention, and intuition to operate for your highest and best purpose.

In his work, Dr. Masaru Emoto discovered that on a molecular level, water crystals are seen to be affected by sound. His water experiments show the effect sound frequencies can have on water, and since our bodies are largely made of water, it is hypothesized that this frequency can have positive benefits on our bodies and minds.

The 417 Hz frequency is another frequency that would be helpful in facilitating the creative capacities of our brains. (Mindfulness Exercises, 2017) This frequency is said to help eliminate negative energy inside us. Because of this, it is said to help bring change and mark the start of new beginnings. With benefits like removing negative energy and thoughts and facilitating change, it can be a powerful help in creative thinking.

In addition to individual ways to build brainpower, there are also group ways to boost our brain capacity. Improvisational comedy warm-up exercises are a great way to get the brainpower of a group going. A typical example is an exercise called "Three Line Scene." It is commonly played with a "Yes, and" rule.

In this exercise, people in the group pair off, and one person in the pair delivers a random statement that is not a question to the other person, such as "I have to pump air into this basketball." The other person has to instantly respond with a line that starts with the words "Yes, and" that builds upon the first person's line, such as "Yes, and I have a flat football here too." The first person instantly responds with another affirming line that starts with "Yes, and," such as "Yes, and footballs make me want to eat chips."

These exercises are great activities for working out that problem-solving lobe and creating neural pathways that our problem-solving lobe can use. These activities can also be quite humorous, which raises the BDNF level in the brain, which in turn gives us heightened neuroplasticity and memory recall of those neural pathways related to solving problems—all good strengths to build for innovation.

There are a many of these kinds of warm-up activities, and volumes have been written on them. I would suggest looking up both *improv* and *brainstorming warm-up activities* at https://www.kablooe.com/

podcasts-webinars-articles-2/brainstormwarmups and use them for ten to fifteen minutes just prior to engaging in your creative problem-solving activity.

One of the most effective ways to launch an ideation effort is with a well-designed and controlled group brainstorming activity. You have heard the saying that the whole is more than the sum of its parts. This phrase is generally attributed to Aristotle. The idea is that when certain entities come together, they are enhanced by what they receive from the other entities and are able to expel more value than they could alone. Not only this, but when you then collect the output of all of these entities working together, you get a larger output than if you were to tally their individual outputs and put them together later. This is due in part to the increased output of each entity when working in a group.

This effect does not exist in all situations. There are many situations where there is a job to be done, and it is pretty much a one-person job. Splitting it up into several tasks with several people would actually slow it down and create a less-cohesive and weaker outcome. One example might be building a 3D CAD file of an individual part on the computer. Every edge, corner, and surface is related to the next as it is created and could not be given to two people to work on at the same time.

Creative-thinking activities are different, however. The concept of building on the ideas of others seems to be a natural occurrence when creative thinking is going on in a group. If we can use math as a model, think of certain situations, like building the CAD file, to be like addition. With addition, the whole in the end is exactly the sum of its parts; four plus four only equals eight, and that is all it will ever equal. But creative problem-solving is more like multiplication. Those same two numbers, four and four, now equal sixteen. Why? Because they have more benefits than just being stacked on top of each other. Each number can be thought of as being used to bring out more than the value of the other number.

So it is with creative thinking. I know there have been many studies and many articles and commentaries written on the subject, including some that have tried to suggest that doing creative work in groups is actually less effective for creative problem-solving than going it alone. In my thirty-five-plus years of product design and development, I can tell you that I have not seen that to be true. I think it is based on a misconception of what creative ideation is. Those who complain that group activities did not work as well had their largest complaints in the area of idea sorting, which is a separate activity and not at all the same thing as the actual creative work to generate the ideas.

Building on the ideas of others is the main strength of brainstorming activities. I have found that this activity can often be quite humorous, which only helps fuel the creative juices as we saw earlier (Czikszentmihalyi, M. 2009). Oftentimes in a brainstorming activity, someone describes an idea, which tends to happen quickly and succinctly. Another member of the group hears what the person is saying but misinterprets the intention of the idea due to the brevity of the explanation, and offers an augmented idea.

There are two levels of multiplication of thought going on here: first, the second person most likely would not have conceived of this augmented idea without the offering of the first person's idea, and secondly would not have constructed the idea as it was given without the misinterpretation of the first idea. Laughter usually ensues upon the discovery of the misconception, but often that misconceived idea gives birth to another idea from a member of the group, and so on.

If you recall, according to the 2010 MIT study, the association of seemingly unrelated items being put together to create an outcome is the core of wit, humor, improvisational comedy, and creative problem solving. An analysis of a group brainstorming activity will reveal that this is precisely what is going on during the activity. Many elements of the design problem seem unrelated, but as group members offer ideas, others see the relatedness of those ideas to certain design problems and make an association. The next person sees that and makes another association, and so on. In this way, we are harnessing our brainpower as a group and discovering that the whole is truly greater than the sum of its parts.

Part Two

A Path to Innovation

Chapter 8

A Broken Process

Most Processes Skip Critical Parts

In 2007, the Institute for Health Technology Studies, in cooperation with researchers at Stanford University, conducted a study to determine the most standard or common development processes among medical-device manufacturers in the United States (Linehan, J., Ph.D. et al., 2007). The processes these companies generally followed were condensed into a process chart, as shown in the stage-gate development chart.

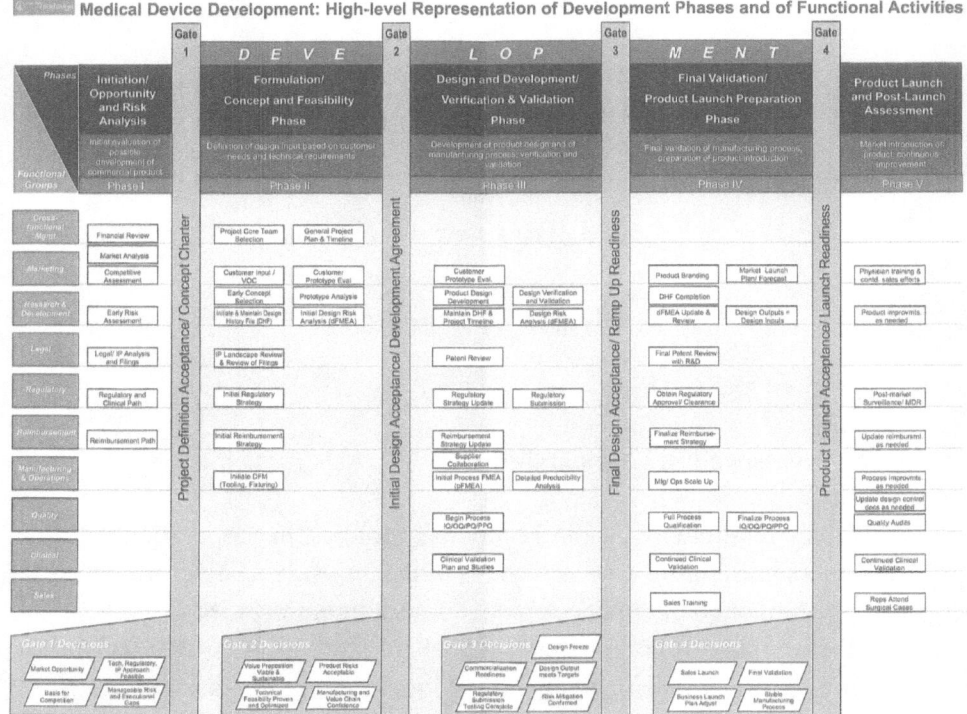

Medical Device Development Process Chart

We can see that all functional groups are listed on the left of the chart (with the exception of *design*), and phases are spread across the x axis. It could be argued that design is really part of the R&D functional group, but upon review of the tasks listed in the body of the chart for R&D, we see very few design items there. This may not be surprising when considering the propensity for new product-development effort failures. This seems to indicate a relationship, showing that a portion of these failures may be due in part to the lack of design discipline in the currently used processes.

Upon inspection, we discover that there are many gaps and missing parts to the current process, the most obvious of which is the complete absence of a design department. The fact that design is tucked in under R&D shows that companies are not using design as the coherent, cross-disciplinary force that leads and drives projects through the development process. In most cases, product companies are using design in a more strike-force-like fashion to do small tasks here and there throughout the process. This leads to design becoming an afterthought in the project, rather than a driving force, in part because nobody really knows who is responsible to foster and drive design into all of the functional groups and phases of the project.

We also see that research and ideation are completely missing from the process, yet prototypes still magically appear and are evaluated. This can have extreme ramifications, as it means that more than likely, the product will have to be designed over and over again several times, consuming large amounts of time and money, and innovation may be completely lacking if the proper creative steps are not engaged to create those prototypes. Additionally, we see that evaluation steps and other development steps are out of order, which will also cause redundancy in the process.

The formulation, concept, and feasibility phase is really too large, and encompasses too many activities in a mixed-up order. This phase needed to be separated into several other phases, which we will see when we examine the improved process. Secondary design steps are also missing or hidden within engineering, which makes them occur too late in the process.

According to Phil Corse, marketing professor at the Kellogg School of Management, one of the major contributing factors to the failure rate of newly designed products is that research is not conducted, it's not conducted effectively, and it is not implemented (Corse P., 2009). Developing a product without doing extensive and proper research is a lot like throwing darts at a dartboard and hoping that you will hit the bull's-eye. However, very few product companies have an aim that is precise enough to accomplish success in this fashion, especially when the target is moving. I remember a classroom discussion once with my colleague Walter Herbst of HLB Design, when he so aptly asserted that "development efforts will fail every time" without ethnographic research and deep immersion into the user space.

Design-Driven Development

I often tell people when giving them instructions for good development processes to not go leaping straight into engineering. It is one of the most common mistakes made in the development world today, especially with medical devices. If we think of engineering as figuring out how to make things work, it would consist of quite a few very detailed and time-consuming tasks related to the ancillary functions of a device. I say *ancillary* because, as we discussed earlier, a technology-related project does need to have the technology vetted and confirmed to a level of confidence before continuing.

I think it is important to understand the contrasts between the disciplines of engineering and design. With engineering, our goal is to figure out how to make things work. With design, our goal is to figure out how to make those things useful for humans. In order to successfully achieve the former, you have to be very focused on acute issues and functions; your attention is on the details that make or break the functionality of the device. With the latter, you have to embrace a broad, holistic approach; in order to make it useful for humans, you have to take into account the needs of users, buyers, manufacturers, assemblers, payors, patients, and peripheral users. This requires a very broad and empathetic mind-set and approach. It can be very different from the mind-set used in the engineering effort.

If you are like me, you are asking yourself, "Why would those two things ever be separated? Why would anyone want to make something that works, but not have it be usable by humans, or make something usable that doesn't work?" The answer is that they wouldn't. Nobody would. If you could ask Leonardo da Vinci, he would agree. He was a man who interwove engineering and design together in almost everything he did. His artistic works rivaled anyone of his time, and his engineering efforts are still admired to this day. He would have never thought of separating those two disciplines.

Yet in our world today, these two disciplines are treated as distinctly different, so we must pay attention to how we handle each one to make sure it is not at the expense of the other, or the innovation project will ultimately suffer in one way or another.

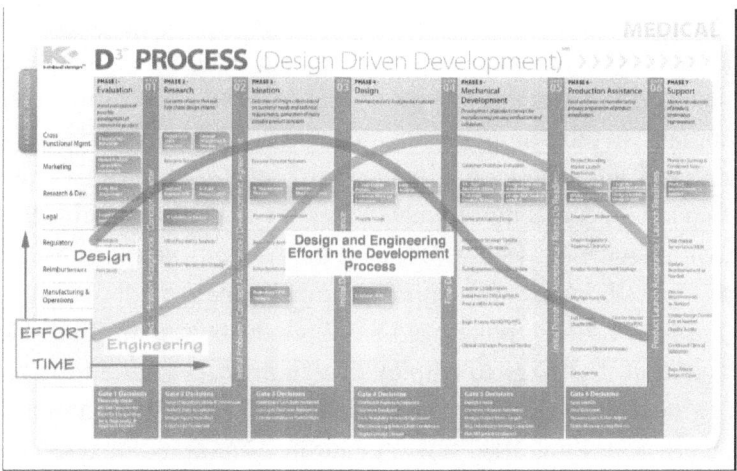

Design and Engineering efforts throughout the development process

To start a development project by leaping into engineering first is to start in the middle of the project. The chart above shows a balanced and recommended approach to the intensity of the workload levels of the disciplines of design and engineering during a typical development project. You can see that design is heavy during the earlier parts of the project and begins to trail off later. Inversely, engineering is lighter in the early phases, although notably it is still there. It reaches its higher levels later in the development process. The exception is if it is a technology project. Then there is a spike in engineering on the front end.

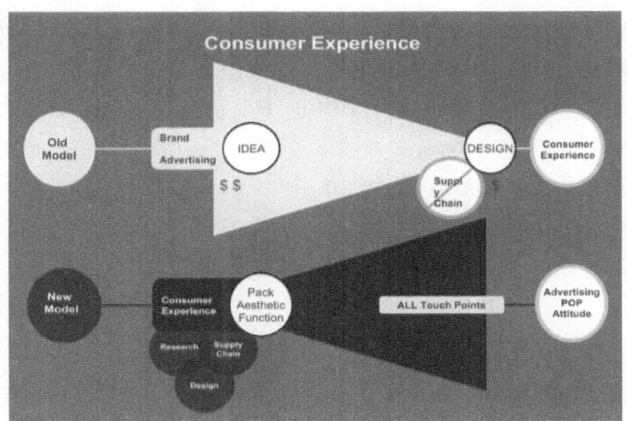

Product Development Methodologies

Mark Dziersk, the late industrial designer, taught in the product management department at the Kellogg School of Management in Chicago. In his teaching, he shared a chart describing product-development methodologies, with an emphasis on heavier design in the earlier phases and heavier engineering in the later phases. His rationale is based on the fact that more time and money is spent on engineering the details of a device or system. If that task is done first and subsequently new information is discovered that warrants a change, it is a costly thing to do it all over, or to make even small changes at that point. He also points out that if you try to employ design practices late in the process after engineering is done, you can have very little effect on the device, and you are pretty much relying on your post-market data to come in to see if you succeeded or if change is necessary.

He contrasts this with an opposing chart that shows design effort in the early phases near the front of a project. The spend in time and money on this work is less, and it informs the team of the requirements for the device, bringing knowledge about what it needs to be. The design effort also does a good job of spotting early those bits of new user information that could warrant a design change in the device. This allows them to be incorporated into the original design, avoiding costly redos later when much engineering time and money has been spent.

In order to execute a successful design effort like this in the early stages of an innovation project, the leaders of your design efforts must be the right kind of people. To successfully achieve a cohesive and holistic design process effort, your leading design thinkers need to be like orchestra conductors. All of the disciplines from the development process chart (marketing, corporate, R&D, manufacturing, etc.) are distinct silos in today's business world, and pulling all the parts together so they are complementing one another to achieve a common purpose is what the maestro does.

Who better to do this than the design thinkers leading the design efforts? They are already trained to take marketing, manufacturing, and other needs into consideration in their work. This person need not always be a designer by training, just a leader who embraces the holistic nature of the user-centered design process and understands its goals and methods. While gathering information about the needs of the key stakeholders in each of these silos, this leader will focus some of the design effort on finding solutions for those needs, as is required in the process. Win-win!

Conductor and orchestra

Only Fools Fall in Love

The problem with leaping straight into engineering early, I believe, stems from the natural human desire to conquer an obstacle quickly. The design challenge is an obstacle, and as soon as we think we have a solution, we get excited about testing it to see if it is a successful solution. This is human nature.

The problem is that we can easily fall in love with our first idea. A kind of pride sets in, and we don't want to see our beloved idea die. We protect it, we fight for it, and usually this goes on far too long and at too great of an expense. It is a time-waster and a money-waster. Early ideas should be logged and then evaluated with the rest of the ideas at the end of the ideation phase. This will allow for the greatest chance of success.

Fail Early, Fail Often, but Fail Smart

The reason this leaping-into-engineering mind-set often causes project failure is because it skips over the ideation process, which is the bedrock of innovation. Lean thinking and agile processes are all reasons people use as excuses for leaping into engineering first. But lean and agile methods actually do not support this leap.

You have probably heard the mantra, "Fail early, fail often." Some use this mantra as an excuse to leap directly into engineering early. However, it would defeat the purpose of the mantra if you did. This is why at Kablooe we developed our own version of this mantra that says, "Fail early, fail often, fail smart." If you are just failing repeatedly but not doing it wisely, you are going to shoot yourself in the foot.

The idea they are trying to push with this mantra is that you should test your ideas early, when it is quick and easy to do so. Then you can learn from them in a rapid and efficient fashion and spend more of your time and money, as Dierszk (2010) recommended, later in the process when your chances of getting it right have already been enhanced by having a good design groundwork laid. This is all very true and supported by our process at Kablooe. The "fail smart" part is an effort to keep people on track with the idea.

If people want to chase down their first idea early in the process because they fell in love with it, and spend time and money engineering it so they can make a prototype to test, they have missed the *smart* part. This is the part that encourages them to test many potential solutions, and to do it in a quick and efficient way—for instance, with quick sketches or rudimentary mock-ups. That is smart. You can then spend engineering time creating the most favorable concepts into higher-end models that can be evaluated at a higher level.

Chapter 9

Finding The Missing Process Parts

Skipped Steps

When we examined the process chart that analyzed how development was being done in 2007, you will remember there were a handful of areas that were glaringly absent. The most notable absentees were:

- discovery phase
- contextual inquiry and ethnographic studies
- brainstorming
- ideation
- concept selection
- mock-ups, usability studies
- design efforts, such as form and ergonomic studies
- visual design language

Does anything on this list look familiar? Remember all of the things we talked about in Part One? It seems that almost every one of them is on this list. If you examine this list closely, you will see that almost everything on it can be considered a right-brain activity. Why is it that the parts of the process that were missing were nearly all right-brain tasks?

The answer might lie in the background of the people who were in charge of the development process. If we look back at the types of people who were instrumental in forming the development path of those companies that were part of the 2007 survey, you would most likely find that the majority of them were VPs or directors of engineering, R&D, or marketing. Most would have an engineering or a business background. There would have been little or no training in the holistic design elements that make a development effort strong and give a strong foundation for innovation.

At the time of that survey, studies were showing that 90 percent of all new product-development efforts were failing. No wonder. They all seemed to be missing all of these things. At Kablooe, this realization sounded an alarm for us to let our customers know that employing these activities might be a huge factor in turning that failure rate around. And as it turned out, we found data showing that it did.

Why Has the Right Brain Been Kicked Out?

I would like to take this moment to lay the blame squarely on Henry Ford's shoulders. Mr. Ford was the man who popularized the use of the assembly line by relying on it to make his factory feasibly produce a product that his target user group could afford. This was no small task, and volumes have been written about it. Without going into a deep history lesson here, suffice it to say that the system he put together was prolific and magnificent. A mistake that our society has made since then is to use the fundamental structures of such a factory and model the education system of our nation after it.

Learning activities were not meant to be compartmentalized the way an assembly line is. As we read earlier with the information given by Sir Ken Robinson, it hasn't been working from a creativity standpoint. Socrates showed us that art, science, literature, math, technology, and the like are all part of being a whole person, but in our academic system today we have compartmentalized our learning and departed from the development of a holistic graduate.

Because engineers can go through their entire undergraduate and graduate programs without ever having their brain touch on an artistic or axiological topic, it is no wonder that as they become the leaders and VPs driving the development processes of our corporations, they have no capacity to consider including the right-brained activities that constitute the early parts of the development process that were ubiquitously missing from the 2007 study. These areas seem to be the missing factor in turning that failure rate around, yet we have no mechanism in our academic structure to bring these areas into the development process from a leadership position.

Medical Device Example: Hospital Purchasing

Let's take a look at an example of how this might play out in the real world with medical devices. Many medical devices are purchased by hospitals based on a favorable decision rendered by a board at the hospital. These boards are often called value analysis committees (VACs).

When a manufacturer has a new device, the VAC will have a review of the device and make a buying decision for the hospital based on a number of factors. These factors can be grouped into about six various areas of importance, consisting of the enormity of the disease burden, the gravity of the unmet need, the ability to bring clinical value, the ability to harness economic value, the likelihood of user and/or patient adherence, and the ability for it to fit within current budget restrictions.

If you and I were developing a new innovative medical device that we wanted hospitals to start purchasing, we would have to structure the steps of our development process. Imagine if we just came up with our first solution to the problem, built a prototype, fell in love with it, and began asking hospitals to buy it. What would the outcome of that effort be? There is a high chance that we could get shot down, and if it wasn't for lack of clinical value, it could very well be for lack of economic value, or a variety of other factors that are important to our buyers that we totally ignored.

Now imagine if we did early studies with our users, watched how they operated, and discovered their needs. Imagine that we interviewed all of the key stakeholders, from the people at the hospital who made the buying decision to the people in the sterilization lab, and even the hospital finance manager. Imagine we took these needs into account and brainstormed with a group of designers, created rough mock-ups, and had them evaluated for usability, then made more refined mock-ups and had them evaluated for usability and function. Then we developed a visual look to the device that relayed the important features and attributes, and we rolled all this knowledge into a final device that incorporated the new technology that we were developing alongside this the whole time. Do you think we might have hit closer to home with patient adherence, budget restrictions, clinical value, and economic value? I think so.

Hospital purchasing is just one example of where this sort of development thinking enhances our ability to succeed. There are other things that are equally important that can be of benefit, such as helping with insurance reimbursement, reducing risks, increasing safety, ensuring the device is more efficacious, increasing user adoption, and enlarging an advantage in the marketplace.

A development process that is missing these steps is a recipe for disaster, continuing to foster the dismal statistics we have seen to this point.

Chapter 10

Process Is Wrong, Right?

Process Order

When most people think of innovation, they think of serendipity. They think of lightning striking with that great idea that nobody else has ever thought of. They think of chance inspiration and a wild, creative, and nonlinear process that is messy and just happens to spin out into a fabulous creative idea. They think of chaos theory, Jeff Goldblum in *Jurassic Park*. They might even think of Bill the "idea man" from *Night Shift*. The last thing many of them think about is logic, order, and process.

In reality, those are exactly what we should be thinking of. Peter Erickson, senior vice president of Innovation at General Mills, once said, "As soon as you put structure and process in place, you don't have creativity. The innovation process and invention process is inherently a creative process that you can't plan for. It's serendipitous. Great ideas just happen, and it is an inefficient process. I contend that this is *not* the case." (Erickson, P. 2009)

This sentiment is also reflected in the writings of Mojanbir Sawhney and Robert Wolcott in their journal article: *Seven Innovation Myths* where they state, "Structure and process do not have to be the enemies of innovation. Just enough structure and process can actually *facilitate* innovation." (Sawhney, M., & Wolcott, R. C., 2004).

Process is our friend, process helps us to not forget important things while we are enamored with shiny, glittery, technological possibilities, or distracted by challenges in our path. Process lays out our tasks in order, and the process we are suggesting in this book includes recurring cycles of reiteration to help us correct errors and move in the best direction. Without process, we are trying to maneuver a raft without a paddle.

Embracing a good, holistic, creative, and iterative process is the key to success, and exactly what I am promoting in this book. I will flesh out this process for you more fully in Chapter 12.

Classic Design vs. Engineering Problems

Because of the classic design and engineering shortcomings in most development work discussed in the previous chapters, there have been some common problems in the development process of device developers over the last several decades. Two of the most common are the tendency to design things that can't be manufactured and engineering devices that lose design intent.

When something is designed that can't be manufactured, it is evidence that there was a breakdown of good development process planning. In a good, holistic development process, this should never occur. Why? Because those manufacturing requirements that are unique to the device and facilitate its production would be part of the design inputs, which are a subset of the product requirements. These design inputs would force the designer to include details into the early design concepts that accommodate these requirements. It would be part of the concept, and designers would be demonstrating the ways this manufacturing would be possible with every design concept submitted … just as they would do with every other design input.

Similarly, with the appropriate development process, an engineer would never lose design intent while detailing the finer aspects of the device's configuration and function. Why? Because the design intent would have been clearly communicated through the previous phases of the process, and the engineering staff would have been part of that development. There would be understanding and ownership of the design intent by the entire staff, both design and engineering. Visual-language strategy would be understood, device configuration for usability would have been developed and tested, and functional configurations would be approved. This all would lead to a smooth transition into engineering and technology and then production.

Wrong Order of Steps

Another common pitfall when design is lacking is to undergo parts of the development process in the wrong order. If the process is started without proper research, or with bad research, then inevitably more research is done later in the project at an inopportune time, which causes all of the steps that should be done after research to be done over again. Oftentimes, a company will start with a concept and become married to it before research is done. This leads to an unfortunate movie-critic syndrome, where after production is finished research data can be gathered, but it is too late to do anything about it other than criticize it.

If engineering is started too early in the process, much time and effort can go into the creation of CAD files and final solutions before the best direction is chosen. Then when research and design factors lead in a different direction, valuable time and resources have already been expended. As you recall, our friend Arthur Fry, inventor of the Post-it Note, stated, "Good product development takes time, and a culture built around design and innovation" in his lecture titled "The Post-it Note Was Not an Accident" (Fry A, 2009). A sufficient amount of time must be spent on the appropriate design activities *before* significant engineering time is spent on a project.

Process Must Include Iterations

People often ask about design iterations when faced with the notion that a process has to be put in place. "If we have a process, how do we accommodate for the inevitability that there will be reiterations to the design of the device?" they wonder.

The answer lies in the inclusion of iterations into each phase of the development process. In the ideation phase, early in the process, we account for large iteration cycles that are completely transforming the device and its attributes. This is very reflective of the nature of the ideation phase. Next, in the design phase, we have fewer concept options, so our iteration cycles are smaller, both in frequency and amplitude. This means that there will more than likely be fewer iterations, because we are more closely honing in on a single design concept, but also that the magnitude of the iterative cycles will not be as large. We are not completely revamping the concept of the device but simply refining some of its attributes.

Finally, in the engineering phase, we have small iterative cycles that are focusing on the smaller details of the device. The device concept remains the same in nature, but small aspects are being refined and defined. If these iterative cycles were visually laid over the top of our development-process chart, we would see larger cycles early on, getting smaller with each phase as they focus on more targeted details.

Chapter 11

Design-Driven Development

Creating a Refined Process

After twenty years of working in the product-development arena, I began to see the need for change, based on many of the things we have discussed so far in this book. After understanding the dismal success statistics of people in our field, I began to understand that development processes had to be led with a different mentality, a different mind-set. This had me grappling with the idea that the best person to devise and lead a development process would be a design thinker with a holistic view of development and the ability to lead a diverse organization, much like the orchestra conductor we described earlier.

It also made me realize that the phases of the process needed to change, and design-oriented tasks that were previously ignored out of inexperience and ignorance needed to be put in. This is what led to the formation of the Design Driven Development Process® (D3 Process®) in 2009.

Directing the Orchestra

Appointing a design-thinker type of person to lead the product-development process across many departmental silos is important, and essential to achieving success with an innovation team. Remember the analogy of the orchestra conductor leading a group of musicians playing different instruments to play a single song with unity? This is what a leader who is a design thinker will do for your innovation effort.

It is the need for a form of holistic thinking in design that makes these people so valuable. As holistic thinkers, they will naturally take into account the needs of all silos of the company, as well as the needs of the various users and stakeholders. This innate brainwork then leads them to create project steps and phases that include activities supporting the creation of solutions for all of these groups, thus drawing them deeper into the process and developing a unity and empathy within the development group for each other's needs. A project leader like this, armed with a complete and holistic process, will be the gateway to a successful product launch at the end of a successful development process.

Phase Breakdowns

With careful consideration to design and its methodologies, revisions have been made to the original process chart to create an improved product-development process. As you will see, this process chart includes many of the previously missing components. First of all, in order to visualize design's involvement across discipline silos and throughout the process, the most directly involved areas of design are shown in the shaded boxes. You can see that design is involved in all seven of the stage gates and is directly involved with activities in five of the functional groups, as well as indirectly in the other five.

You can see that this makes the design discipline the logical choice to lead the project and provide the project champion as a leader guide. Unfortunately, this is rarely the case in business today. Most product companies do not have a holistic view of design or its practices and therefore miss out on the opportunity to use it throughout the process and as a driver to keep the process on track. A good design team or independent designer will possess the necessary skills and talents to drive this holistic process.

Next, you will see that the first phase between gates one and two has been broken into two phases: Research and Ideation. Research requires activity from six of the ten functional groups, with a possible seventh being manufacturing. The phase between gates two and three in the existing process has also been broken into two phases: Design and Engineering. With the addition of these elements, the new process now consists of seven phases and six phase gates, where *go* or *no-go* decisions are made regarding moving to the next phase.

The increased number of phases decreases the amount of risk involved. Much like any gambling endeavor, as the risk goes down, the spending and investment can go up, which allows more time and resources to be spent on a project as it progresses. The *go* or *no-go* phase gates allow this to happen. As it is now defined in this new model, there are seven phases to the development process.

Benefits

There are many benefits to a development process of this structure, several of which I would like to point out here.

First, there is the advantage of the information derived from the design research. Not only is this information used to inform the design process, but with medical devices it can also be used as formative study data in the Human Factors Engineering (HFE) file. Formative studies are investigations into the usability of the device to gather information that will be used to further direct the design of the device. These studies can be very informal, and although there are good descriptive models for these studies in the guidance literature, from a regulatory standpoint, they can be fairly loosely designed. The goal is just to show that information was discovered that positively impacted the design of the device. Instead of spending time and money on separate studies, the design research effort and HFE effort can share the same study, and both can benefit from the data and information gained.

Second, it can be very beneficial to do mini versions of tasks that occur later in the process in these earlier phases. For instance, one of the things required in a risk-management plan is a design failure mode and effects analysis (DFMEA). When designers are doing early design research and formative studies, they can begin postulating what could go wrong with the device usage and what could be done to mitigate it. Simply recording these thoughts and putting them in a chart to analyze later is the beginning of DFMEA thinking. Likewise, design for manufacturing (DFM), design for assembly (DFA), and risk analysis are all things that come later in the process but can have mini versions kicked off in these early phases that will inevitably inform the design effort and streamline the later analysis tasks.

Another benefit is user input. The process is designed to have many places for user input. The prototypes increase in complexity as the process progresses, and user feedback is gained along the way with increasing fidelity. This user input is critical to help define the product requirements and inform the design effort continually throughout the process.

In the research phase, we are getting feedback from users without even having a prototype. We observe them using current devices and methods to meet their needs, and we draw conclusions about how those needs may or may not be getting adequately met. In the subsequent ideation phase, we use rough mock-ups for quick feedback with a large number of concepts, and reduce the number of concepts and refine the quality of the prototypes as the phase moves forward, usually through about three or so rounds of prototypes and testing.

Then, in the design and engineering phases, we introduce more refined prototypes and get very detailed input from users and approvals from project leaders. This is a coordinated effort that involves strong design leadership to construct the studies, undertake the research, and define the appropriate changes and improvements that will result.

Another great benefit of a process like this is the ability to use the design research data from the early phases in risk-analysis activities. As we stated before, most medical devices will be required to have a risk-management plan, and many nonmedical devices will employ a risk-management plan as well. Because the nature of design research is to find out how users respond to the device, its use, and the environment and situations that it is used in, oftentimes information regarding actions that create risks and possibly lead to hazards is discovered. Because the D3 Process® does this in a very unique and robust way, there is often a large amount of relevant data that can be fed into risk-management activities. Much like the human-factors work and the formative studies, these efficiencies can save considerable time and cost.

These design research tasks can also support marketing activities, inform corporate decisions, and guide intellectual property pathways. This is another way that we see the holistic nature of the design process as it supports so many other disciplines around it, making it the one discipline that seems to really tie many of the others together.

What is the magic here? Remember the three major areas of the brain involved in creativity, and how they switch from daydreaming to focused activity? This is how your brain was designed to be creative, and we have already established that innovating is a creative problem-solving activity. The innovation process I am describing here reflects that same pattern your brain is using during creativity. There are phases of wondering and seeking, followed by phases of focused attention to making things work. Then more wondering and seeking regarding the new learnings, again followed by focused activity to describe working solutions.

This kind of activity is sometimes referred to as "sprints" related to agile development techniques, but here this pattern is repeated in a more refined manner with each iteration, building upon itself with careful attention to the early research and brainstorming stages to ensure that too much time and energy is not put into one concept before a plethora of others are explored. In this way, we are truly innovating the way our brains were designed to conceive of innovations.

So what do these phases look like and what actual activities do we undertake in each one? Let's discuss that in the next chapter.

Chapter 12

Phase Descriptions

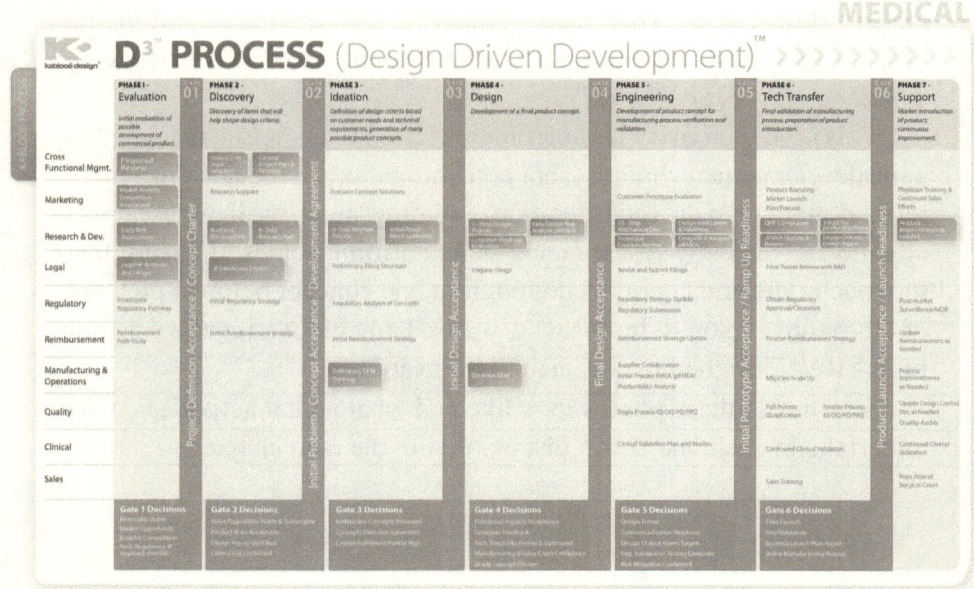

The D3 Process®: Design Driven Development®

As mentioned before, we took the development process and separated it into seven phases. Each phase is populated with necessary tasks from each of the ten functional groups of workers, commonly called silos. Here we will take a detailed look at each of those seven phases and the major tasks in each phase in the R&D silo. Volumes could be written on the tasks in each of the phases for all of the other silos, but because this book is focused on design and engineering, the R&D silo path is the one we will investigate.

D3 Process® Phase 1: Evaluation

The first phase is titled *evaluation*. In this phase, we are attempting an initial evaluation of the possible development of a commercial product. This evaluation serves the purpose of informing a decision to undertake the effort at all, and it is extremely important from a financial and intellectual property perspective. If the legal team and the finance team can see a viable path forward, the momentum to continue is high. This phase is often called a *vetting* phase, and groups like the Carlson School of Management have courses in developing good vetting techniques for product-development projects.

The discovery phase in the D3 Process®, however, is a bit deeper with its investigations than a standard vetting process. Some of the major decisions coming from this phase to determine if the project should initiate are the determination that there is financial viability, a reasonable market opportunity, a decent basis for competition, and a reasonable assurance of a feasible approach to technology, intellectual property, and regulatory hurdles.

Some of the activities going on during this phase in the silos other than R&D are financial reviews; early market analysis and competitive assessments; analysis of the legal and patent landscape; investigation into regulatory pathways; and reimbursement opportunities. The actual goal of this phase is to help innovators choose their projects wisely. The activities in this phase represent a preliminary, yet comprehensive, investigation into critical factors that will contribute to the project's success. Once this work is done, innovators can focus on deeper specific vetting activities prescribed by their financial and legal teams. From there, they can go even deeper and develop a full business plan that could be suitable for courting venture money and similar strategic financing options.

Here is the curious thing about the evaluation phase: its activities prescribed below are for the R&D team to execute. Yes, even though we have financial, legal, and other activities that would likely be thought of as being executed by groups in the other silos outside of R&D, we are suggesting that the R&D team execute these activities. Why? Because each of these tasks I will be describing is a first attempt, an early dive if you will, into the subject matter. This helps inform the development team, and an informed R&D team is a strong, wise, and efficient R&D team. Besides, they can do this early preliminary work at a fraction of the cost of legal and marketing teams.

Step 1: Financial Review

The first and probably most important thing you need to do in the evaluation phase is start with a financial review. There are six major areas of investigation to look at in this phase that can help render a *go* or *no-go* decision on the project from a financial perspective:

1. Size of Market

First, you need to estimate the size of the market. Pie-in-the-sky gigantic market-size estimates do you no good here. You need to be realistic. Look at the worst possible scenario for market size. Remember, you are doing this step to make sure you are on the right path or if you will be throwing your time and money away. You need to know the answer in either case.

Consider the potential patient population (search hcupnet.gov using ICD-9 codes and literature introduction sections). Additionally, gather info on competitor product sales histories, or even look at industry analysis that could reveal information for units sold and market revenue (search investor reports or hoovers.com if private). Find out how much of the market has been penetrated now with the current devices or systems that are being used by the market to cope with the problem you will be attempting to solve with your potential product or system.

2. Impact of Idea on Market

Is your device a great idea? You probably think so. But your opinion can be skewed by your passion and love for your idea. To combat this, you need to assess the impact of the idea on the market. Ask yourself if there is a real need for this innovation, and then search among your intended user groups to see if there is chatter to support your hunch.

Is this a disruptive technology, or does it fit within an existing product platform? That will make a difference to the scope of your development project. Investigate why current products fall short of total user acceptance if they do. Then quantify these current device failed outcomes and determine the cost of failures. This will help you understand whether the difference your idea could make would be noticed or thought of as worthwhile by your intended user group.

3. Potential Return on Investment

What are the fixed, semi-fixed, and variable costs of development (including regulatory costs, IP costs, and R&D expenses)? If you don't know, you need to do a little investigation to find out. You can investigate similar or analogous devices, learn their development stories, and discover what the spend was for them. Assess the unit price for any existing technologies that are similar or analogous and the unit price for the proposed innovation. With this information and the potential market size that you figured earlier, you should be able to estimate the potential return on investment.

4. Cost-Effectiveness Potential

To determine this, you need to identify a potential outcome from the use of your innovations and make a realistic but hypothetical guess at measuring that outcome. You can use analogous devices or system data to extrapolate these numbers. Then you have to estimate your costs to achieve that outcome and divide the cost by the outcome. Evaluate the result and try to determine if that cost will be acceptable to buyers and manufacturers, considering their cost limits. You can then try to pre-identify specific designable elements that may increase the cost-effectiveness numbers.

This is also a good time to define a value proposition. Once you know the cost-effectiveness, you can begin to talk about the value the innovation may bring in terms of lives saved, quality of life, or even other nonmeasurable factors like happiness or life enrichment. These values can be used to balance or offset any disparity in the cost-effectiveness numbers.

5. Reimbursement

If your innovation will potentially be a medical device, you need to think about how insurance may or may not pay for it. This can be a make-or-break detail with medical devices. Insurance companies use a system of codes to classify devices for reimbursement by insurance. Reimbursement can be a very deep and detailed area, and is also one of those areas that volumes have been written on. We will not go into all of those deep details about the reimbursement system here but will focus on the fact that when considering reimbursement, you need to investigate to find if the innovation potentially fits into an existing pathway or if it requires a new one.

Getting a new reimbursement code to cover your device can be a long drawn-out process, potentially taking years, then only to find that it was denied a new reimbursement code. To help you determine this, you need to identify ICD-9 diagnosis and any HCPCS codes that might apply to your device. You also need to identify CPT procedure codes and any associated monetary values.

Ask yourself, "Will this product fit into any existing DRGs?" And "Does it have any special designations (such as a durable medical goods)?" Look for Medicare and private payers' statements on existing procedures. Start the process early. If establishing a new CPT code, you should try to parallel studies with FDA-required trials.

6. Financing

Determining a financing plan with milestones and a budget is a necessity. Of course, at this preliminary stage of the process, the plan and budget are an educated guess. Nevertheless, they are crucial in helping to determine whether a path forward is viable. In this stage, it is helpful to detail out an estimated timeline, complete with FDA, IP, regulatory, R&D, manufacturing, and marketing costs and dates. This can be very difficult at this stage, but again, educated guesses based on data acquired from the previous steps can go a long way.

You can also project a go-to market strategy and date range for the execution of it. Then you can show it to marketing/product-launch consultants and see what they would charge to execute it, after which you can lay out all these activities and associated costs in your financing plan. Consider weighted average cost of capital if borrowing, which means including all of the costs of acquiring and paying back capital. You can use the net present value (NPV) chart below as a template to help determine some of these costs.

Net Present Value Chart

Device/Technology Name			Variable Assumptions		
Incidence of Usage	3,800,000		Unit Sales Price		55.00
			Cost to Manufacture		40.00
			WACC		40.00%
Total	**3,800,000**		Kits per Pt.		1.00

	Year 1	Year 2	Year 3	Year 4	Year 4
Market Share	-	0.00%	0.50%	1.00%	2.00%
Units sold	-	-	19,000	38,000	76,000
Units required	100	500			
Revenue	-	$0	$1,045,000	$2,090,000	$4,180,000
IP	$25,000				
Cost to Manufacture	$4,000	$20,000	$760,000	$1,520,000	$3,040,000
R&D	$100,000	$50,000			
510(k) Trial	$100,000	$150,000	-	-	-
Total Cost	**$204,000**	**$220,000**	**$760,000**	**$1,520,000**	**$3,040,000**
Profit	**-$204,000**	**-$220,000**	**$285,000**	**$570,000**	**$1,140,000**
Net Present Value (NPV)	**$288,743**				

Net Present Value (NPV) worksheet

The goal here is to have a financing plan that you could hand to an investment bank, venture capital group, or angel investment group to get feedback on the reality of your financial assumptions. This will help you determine if there is a financial path that is feasible for your innovation project.

Step 2: Market Analysis

Closely linked to the financial review is a review of the market situation. A brief market analysis recommended by the D3 Process® at this point consists of six areas of investigation:

1. Incidence/Prevalence

If your innovation is a medical device, you need to break down market sizing into incidence and prevalence of the medical indication for your device. *Incidence* is the key data point for market sizing (use hcupnet.gov, census data, and literature to determine this). If your innovation is not a medical device, it is still important to find numbers for these two markers. Briefly put, incidence is the number of people in a given time period (usually per year) who will be put into a situation that can constitute a need for the use of your innovation. Precedence refers to the number of people who are already in that situation from previous years, accumulated to the present.

Knowing these numbers is critical to calculating the number of units you may be able to sell each year. With medical devices, you can usually find fairly readily data regarding people suffering with various conditions. With a nonmedical innovation, it will just require good old-fashioned research to try to find these numbers, and a little creativity helps in finding good places to look for data.

2. Market Penetration

How are you going to penetrate the market you just defined? Even with the best possible marketing plan, how do you know how much of the market will convert to the use of your innovation over other options?

You may think every user will because your device is so much better. But how will they know that, and will they believe it? If they do, will they be willing to pay for it? And even if they are, how many just have the personality that makes them wait to see if others successfully convert to the use of it first?

All of these things are determining factors in calculating market penetration, and you need to find ways to estimate answers to all of these questions, even if they are educated guesses based on past histories of other devices. You have to start with something, then you can improve and refine as you collect better data. Use these items to determine the market penetration potential for your innovation, and look for previous examples that you can use as reference.

3. Key Stakeholders/Users

It is important to know who your key stakeholders and users are. A key stakeholder is anyone who has a vested interest in the use of the device, even if not an actual user. As an example, in a medical-device situation, the stakeholders and users of a device could be patients, physicians, nurses, technicians, specialists, inventory controllers, purchasers, decision-makers, supply-chain people, and payers. You have to consider which of these would be involved with the purchasing and usage of your innovation, and to what extent they could influence both of those areas. Once you understand who each of them is and the role they could play in the life of your device, you are ready to consider the next area of investigation.

4. Barriers to Adoption

Once you know who the stakeholders and users are, you need to find out what the barriers to adoption of the device might be for each of them. This can be hard to find and will take some investigation, most likely including very qualitative methods of research, such as interviews and observations. Barriers can often be hidden-motive types of things. For instance, will your device make a process easier, faster, and cheaper? If so, do users benefit from the current inefficient method because they get paid for their usage of the device by the hour? If so, those users may have a strong disincentive to purchase your device, knowing it could have a negative impact on the financial bottom line of their business. It is good to know these things up front and plan a strategy in the features and configuration of your device that takes them into account.

5. Costing

What can the innovation be sold for at the unit price? You can make some guesses, but it is more important to quantify this with relevant examples of what the market will bear, from competitive devices or similar examples. If it looks like this price is being forced to be lower than necessary for a reasonable return based on the cost structures you estimated earlier, you may have a no-go on your hands.

On the other hand, you need to ascertain if these pricing barriers are only applicable to you as a manufacturer, and determine if there are other manufacturers out there who could achieve a better revenue with a lower manufacturing cost, and if so, if they would be good candidates for acquiring the business or technology. This is a viable exit strategy, and you need to investigate to see if there are multiple possibilities like this in the market. Licensing agreements are worth considering here as well if there are strategic partner companies who live within a more favorable costing environment than you could with a startup company.

6. Timing

It is a good idea to create a preliminary development timeline. You can then pair this with financing structures and options. How long will it take to bring the product to market? Will multiple rounds of fundraising be necessary? Find answers to these questions and plug them into your timeline. Then see if you can find out if there is a window of time in which the market need for this innovation will be relevant.

Windows can be formed by potential releases of competitive devices; legal and regulatory rulings; payment and reimbursement issues; and financing availability. This timeline will help you determine if it will take too long to hit the market in time to meet the need. If it will, you need to determine if there are ways you can shorten your go-to-market timing, or you may again have a no-go on your hands.

Step 3: Competitive Assessment

The next major step in evaluating the opportunity potential for your innovation is to size up the competition. You have already done a bit of this in the first two steps, but now it's time to dig a little deeper. Here are five important areas of investigation involved in sizing up the competition:

1. Identify the Competition

Now you have to identify who all the competitors are that are already active in the marketplace. Make a list. Dig deep. Don't miss anybody, big or small. The small ones might be an up-and-coming threat. You should also dig into each of these competitors' activities to see what products are coming through their pipelines. Do they have more than one model? Do they have ancillary, peripheral, supportive product lines?

Knowing these things will help you identify the strength of the competition in terms of lifespan, customer loyalty, market share, and dilution of market share per player. Once you know who they are and how they are operating, you can move into the next four areas of investigation.

2. Sales Threats

Now you need to find out what your competitors' stakes are in the market. Break down each competitor's presence in terms of percentage of market share and dilution of the market. This data can be difficult to find directly, but you may be able to access copies of annual reports or marketing presentations that can give you a good idea.

Remember, at this early phase, it is still all preliminary data. It is easy to identify the competitor with the largest market share as your biggest sales threat, but that is not always the case. Sometimes those companies are very comfortable with their large lead in the market and have no incentive to spend money making changes.

Also, companies with smaller market share may be up and coming, with new features and attractive benefits for users, and may be working with a hunger to unseat the larger market players. Assess your discoveries of their product lines to see if you can identify who the biggest threat is and why.

3. Profitability

What is the profitability of competitive devices? Are they all going broke trying to compete in this market? That would be a bad sign. You might believe that your innovation is different, and yours will succeed where everyone else has failed. Maybe so, but why? Are you sure? If you have very positive results from your D3® evaluation phase thus far, maybe you will.

If the competition is not profitable, can you find out why? We are talking about good old-fashioned research here. There are no magic bullets I can give you for finding this out. Although, if the competitors are public companies, there are SCC filings that can be accessed and can give clues to the activities and financial dealings of the companies, as well as annual reports and quarterly earnings. If you know they are building foreign factories, that might explain why cash is tight and financial decisions are being made.

The bottom line is, you need to know if participants are getting healthy in this market or if it is stagnating, which could bode poorly for a new entrant but also create opportunity for that entrant to disrupt the market if an innovation meets user needs in a new way.

4. Advantages

Now you want to list the advantages that you see your innovation will have over the competitors. Will these advantages be enough to overcome difficulties in the market? If so, why? Weigh those advantages against all of the market and competitive data you have so far to see if you have a comfortable case for continuing.

If you are worried that you are too biased toward the innovation to be objective with that analysis, show the information you have so far with a description of your innovation to a willing investor and see what that person thinks about your innovative advantages versus market difficulties. This opinion might be that of only one person, but someone who represents a body of other investors. Take this input as a chance to rethink, revamp, and improve your approach.

5. Outcomes

Is your device going to cause users to have better outcomes than the competitors' devices will? If it is a medical device, will the outcome be better for patients, physicians, hospitals, manufacturing, technology folks, or key stakeholders? If so, how? You will need to think this through and clearly explain why it might be the case in any of these areas. This can be used as weight in any of your cost-effectiveness-potential models.

Step 4: Strategy Risk Assessment

Another important area to size up is the potential risk to your entire strategy and plan to move this forward and bring it to market. Here are eight areas of investigation to think about in order to confirm the risks to your strategy are acceptable

1. Ease of Adoption

Similar to the barriers you evaluated earlier, you now need to determine and rate how easy or hard it might be for users and key stakeholders to adopt your innovation into their world. Does the innovation pose any additional barriers, or does it remove some of the barriers you may have discovered earlier for sellers, buyers, distributors, or manufacturers? It is not enough to show that barriers have been removed. Without obvious barriers, there still might be things that make adoption by users and stakeholders difficult. What if physicians are the buyers and actual users, but patients react poorly to the device? What if the users show no actual barriers in early studies, but after purchasing they have trouble with use or setup and find the device cumbersome in real-world use, when that was unforeseen in early investigations?

You may be injecting a new device into a field where people historically just don't switch devices much, and you don't know why. If any of these types of things can be discovered early, you want to try to identify them here.

2. Credibility

It is important to qualitatively assess the belief of end users and stakeholders in the innovation's viability. The credibility of the enterprise is crucial in a number of different ways, and credibility needs to be achieved in all of these areas.

The first, and perhaps the most important, is the credibility of you and your team to have the expertise and experience to pull off this endeavor from a technological level and a business level. The stakeholders you will need to bring in and work with won't get on board if they don't think you and your team can actually develop this technology and make it work. They will also be hesitant if they think there is a chance that you don't have the chops to manage the business well and are likely to drive it into the ground, even if you can develop the technology appropriately. The experience, training and knowledge shown by your team will go a long way in alleviating these fears and building credibility in these areas.

There is also the need for credibility in your infrastructure. If your innovation will rely on buyers to carry an inventory of your goods, those buyers need to be convinced that your enterprise has the ability to deliver the quantities they need when they need them. Without this credibility, your sales would be dismal.

The need for this kind of credibility really translates into every area of your enterprise. Investors need to be assured that you can create a reasonable return on their investment, manufacturers need to know you can pay your bills, and so on.

This early evaluation stage is a good time to estimate what your team may be like, and what the overall credibility of the team and enterprise will be as you see it now. Then you can outline what can be done to increase credibility in all of these areas and take action in future phases.

3. Complexity

Is the device simple or complex in terms of manufacturing and usability? Using the simple chart below can give you a glimpse into the challenges you may have ahead based on the complexity of the device and the overall endeavor. Will it take scientific research to prove some hypothesis in order to make your innovation work as intended? That dictates a potential high process complexity. Is the science and technology known, but it will require advanced custom circuitry and information processing? That would also dictate a high process complexity. Does the device have a large number of moving parts that all mechanically interact with each other? Or will the adoption of your device require a large educational effort for users?

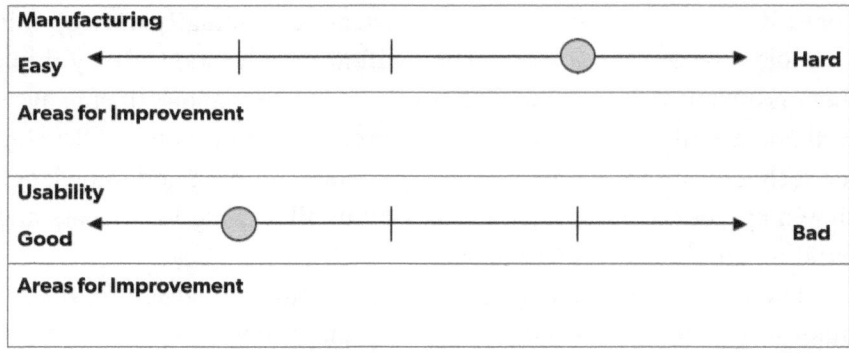

Project Complexity

Items like these can all lead to high levels of complexity in your development process. It is good to estimate these things now so you can ask yourself what can be done to simplify the product, its development, and its ecosystem for use.

4. Technology Risk

This is also the right time to assess the viability of the proposed innovation technologies. Is there a risk that they may not be able to be developed as planned? If they can be, will it be a long period of technological development with a large amount of specialty testing?

Existing technology to be used should be evaluated as well. Specifically, investigate the longevity, supply, cost, and availability of each technological component you may need. These can include things like electronic displays, processors, circuit board components, motors, and pumps.

5. Future Supporting Product Line

Are future iterations of the innovation possible? This can give credibility to your enterprise and reduce risk of failure by offering several potential paths to success. Identify any potential pivot strategies in this step that may involve peripheral and supporting products, next-generation or different-version devices, and potential supporting product lines.

6. Exit-Strategy Risks

Before you can identify risks in your exit strategy, you need to define which exit strategies seem to be viable for your enterprise. These can include options like:

- a company purchase or stock buyout
- the purchase of some or all of your intellectual property
- the licensing of intellectual property or manufacturing rights
- exclusive sales contracts
- continuing to run the company and generate your own sales and revenue

Here you need to identify all realistic, viable options and identify realistic buyout partners and licensing opportunities. Then you need to evaluate which of these options might carry a higher risk of failure than others and why. When your business plan is developed, you can then focus on the exit strategy that presents the least risk with the highest potential gain that most closely meets your enterprise goals.

7. Core Strength Alignment

How does the product align with the company's core strengths? Your so-called "company" most likely won't even really exist in an operational form at this point. It is most likely just a plan or vision for a company, but you need to make some realistic estimates regarding what that company will mostly look like when it is formed. Then you can assess its strengths. For instance:

- Will you have a strong ability to bring in financing?
- Will you have development muscle?
- Will there be a high level of knowledge in your technology area?
- Will you be manufacturing gurus in the methods that are needed for the device?

These are all possible core strengths of your enterprise, and the big question here is whether any or all of these core strengths align with important features and necessary paths for your innovation. If not, this can present a weakness and a higher risk level for your development success, and changing your core strengths or your device attributes to more closely match should be considered at this point.

8. Device Risk Assessment

This investigation revolves around your actual device or system. What kinds of risks could it introduce to the users or environments it is used in? One great way to look at this is to make an early, rough, preliminary attempt at a failure modes and effects analysis (FMEA) for each critical element of the innovation. Executing an FMEA is another one of those areas of study that could be a complete training course of its own, and we won't go into all the details for completing one here. You can look up instructions easily and download some templates to use.

Even though the device is not developed yet, you can run through a preliminary FMEA to give yourself some early warnings for risk areas that you know you can then focus on mitigating in the development process. If you are having trouble identifying risk-mitigation strategies, a higher level of overall risk will be felt by the key stakeholders and could hamper your development plans and support.

Step 5: Legal Activity

Taking a look at legal issues is important at this stage as well. We are recommending here that you take an initial look at these issues yourself, without the input or cost of an actual legal team at this point. What you and your R&D team find can give you some direction for focusing your early efforts and provide a jump start for your legal team once they begin their work. Here are six areas you can focus on investigating at this point.

1. Intellectual Property Landscape

The first thing you need to do is find out who is possibly using intellectual property to protect the exact thing you are thinking of making; who is protecting something similar; and who your competitors are and what they are protecting. I am amazed by how many entrepreneurs I talk with who are convinced no one has thought of the innovation they are thinking about, and during my first conversation with them I Google the subject, find a product exactly like the one they are considering, and ask, "Have you checked out this company to see what their patents cover?" At that point, I am hoping they have not sunk too much money into the concept.

This is the time to create a high-level assessment of the intellectual property landscape. Is the space wide open or cluttered? It is also beneficial to search outside the specific field of the innovation for non-field-related concepts and patentable elements. Google patents and USPTO.gov are great places to do keyword searches to find out what you are dealing with.

Remember, just because a company or product can't be found on Google or Amazon doesn't mean that nobody has patent protection covering it. Inversely, you might find products out there on the market that are close or identical, but they may not have the patent protection they need to keep you from competing for their customer base.

2. Protection

The legal protection you are investigating has many facets you need to consider. The first is protection. Is your potential innovation likely to have protectable features? Do those features satisfy the three criteria for a new patent protection: novel, non-obvious, and useful? If so, then you know that you may have something that can be protected from others who would want to sell the exact same thing. But you don't yet know if you are free to protect those aspects of the innovation.

3. Necessity

It is worth discovering whether intellectual property protection is even necessary for your innovation's profitability, exit strategy, or safety. Some items are best served by just maintaining trade secrets of their makeup. Others may be better served by licensing intellectual property from someone who already has an issued patent. Sometimes a design patent is all you need, and other times a utility patent is necessary.

You can try to determine these needs yourself by analyzing the important aspects of your innovation and investigating what others have done successfully in similar situations. However, a short conversation with an experienced patent attorney may be worthwhile at this point too. You may be in an industry where acquisition is only valued if there is a nice patent portfolio that goes with it. These things are good to consider when deciding what intellectual property path might be the most appropriate for achieving your exit-strategy goals.

4. Obviation

This is where you want to find out if it would be necessary to obviate existing IP, or easy for others to obviate any patent protection you think you might obtain. Identify inventors with existing patents in the space and see if they own the patents, or are an inventor working on behalf of a large company that is the patent assignee. This will help you determine if it could be easy to license from them.

It is also a good time to see if there are any patent trolls to be cautious of. These are groups that watch for old patents and purchase them when they see someone might be violating them and then threaten to prosecute. It is just something to be aware of so you can look deeper when you investigate legal action. Determine if your device would have "freedom to operate," meaning there would be no existing patent claims that yours might hinge on in order to be manufactured, sold, and used.

5. Investigation

This is an activity that is simply looking for what we call the "white space" for the innovation to make unique claims in. It involves reading the claims of the patents of similar devices and understanding what isn't being claimed as novel and protected by the competitive devices. This gives you a playground to work within, knowing that if you keep creating your innovative features in a way that the claims to protect them fall into this playground area, you will be able to get patent protection.

6. Legal Action

Now you want to know if anyone has been sued in this innovation area, and if so, why? This might be where you see some activity from patent trolls, or discover two companies fighting over similar claims. This investigation may also reveal which company tends to be the serial litigator in the space and warrant a careful investigation of their claims on your part.

Basically, you want to learn from the mistakes of others and avoid them in your path to developing your innovation for manufacturing and market release.

Step 6: Regulatory/Reimbursement

The last area you need to spend some significant time in during this early evaluation phase applies only if your innovation is a medical device. Given the fact that patients rely on insurance to pay for many of their devices and procedures, and that the industry is regulated by the FDA in the United States, understanding the requirements necessary to succeed in these two areas is critical.

You will most likely need to engage the services of regulatory and reimbursement experts early on in your journey. However, this work is for you.to develop some ideas in your mind of the feasibility, magnitude, and complexity of the path that lies ahead in order for your innovation to get developed. There are five major areas you should consider at this point.

1. Regulatory Path Identification

For the sake of ease, we will just focus on the FDA when we address regulatory issues here, even though the European Union uses CE marking for regulatory approvals, and other regions have unique systems as well. The first thing you need to do is establish the necessary regulatory path for your innovation. There are a number of options, the most common being Class I exempt, DeNovo, Class II 510(k), and Class III PMA. You will need to look up the requirements for each and determine which path is appropriate for your device. See http://www.fda.gov/downloads/ MedicalDevices/DeviceRegulationandGuidance/GuidanceDocuments/ ucm072701.pdf for help in making this determination.

2. Regulatory Path Options

Here you want to think about options. If you made some changes to the configuration of functionality of your innovation, could that change your regulatory requirements? Are other regulatory paths available? Does the innovation require FDA approval, or can it be marketed without making medical claims at all? If it does require FDA approval, could the concept be modified to make it exempt, or is a 510(k) or a PMA inevitable? You need to know this to prepare a plan that you can stick to and use for fundraising rationale.

3. Device Classification

You need to classify your device first before you can develop your regulatory pathway. A Class I device poses little or no harm to a patient. A Class II device is considered a bit more dangerous, and Class III devices are implantable and surgical items that carry a high risk with their usage. Understanding the class of your innovation will help you identify and estimate clinical trial times and expenses, because the rigor with which tests are done increases with the class of the device.

4. Code Identification and Payment Amounts

Now you need to do a little reimbursement work. Because insurance companies and Medicare pay for these devices and procedures, they have requirements that you need to be aware of. Does the innovation potentially fit into an existing pathway, or does it require a new one? You will need to do the following:

- identify ICD-9 diagnosis and any HCPCS codes
- identify CPT procedure codes and any associated monetary values
- have an understanding of whether or not this product will fit into any existing DRGs
- determine whether your device has any special designations (such as a durable medical good)

All of this information will begin to shape the framework for your financial models, which is a must before you begin to launch into the next steps of your development journey. Start the process early, because if you have to establish a new CPT code, your costs and development times will likely increase.

5. Payer Histories

Identify the billing practices of hospitals (or other entities) on existing competitor products. Look for Medicare and private payers' statements on existing procedures. This will help you determine the realities surrounding your financial model and will suggest the depth of effort necessary if changes need to be made to that model in order for your innovation to thrive.

All of these activities should give you a good sense of security for entering the next phase and provide assurance of good financial viability; substantial and accessible market opportunities; a viable basis for competition; and a high level of assurance of technological, regulatory, and patent paths that are feasible.

D3 Process® Phase 2: Discovery

Congratulations! You have gone through the steps of the D3 Process® evaluation phase and determined it is wise to continue with your innovation project. Now it is essential that you move into the discovery phase of the process. In this phase, you are really doing what I call *design research*. My definition of this is really just doing everything you can to gather enough data to make informed decisions about the design of the device. That's it.

Sounds simple, right? There are many ways you could try to tackle this task, and I would like to share with you what I have found over the years to be the richest and most robust way of gathering this information in order to get good, actionable intel from it.

First of all, you have to understand that the reason you are undertaking these discovery activities is to develop criteria you will use to design your device. One of the biggest myths in product development is that innovation starts with an idea. The truth is that innovation begins with the collection of all the criteria that will be used to judge the value of an idea. So this is how we start innovating: by gathering design criteria.

Design criteria are meant to be turned into requirements, and most product projects have an official requirements document. This document can contain many types of requirements for your innovation, including business, manufacturing, user, marketing, design, financial, and functional requirements. Because we are only focusing on the R&D silo track of the D3 Process®, our focus here for gathering criteria for the formation of requirements will be limited to user and design requirements, with the inclusion of some marketing and costing requirements that support the formation of user and design requirements.

The most common way people try to gather the data they need for forming requirements is from voice of customer (VOC) data. The problem with this is that VOC data can be very weak. Oftentimes, the gathering of VOC data is left to members of the marketing team who may not have a deep enough vision into the tasks of the R&D group and therefore employ methods that fall short of getting useful data.

Asking users what they would like to see improved on the device is just asking them to freeze under pressure and perhaps offer you any suggestion in order to get unfrozen, without regard to the depth of any real need behind the suggestion. Most often this type of criteria is needed before a concept device has been developed, and no prototypes exist yet for preference testing. This leaves many researchers without a clue as to what methods to employ to gain insights and gather data.

Good design research employs techniques that go deep into the psyche and explore the needs of the user, many of which are unable to be articulated by those users. One way of doing this is to analyze your users through the lens of the eight universal job steps. Tony Ulwick of Stratagyn popularized this idea by using these job steps to help companies develop their product portfolios. The idea is from the "Jobs to Be Done" theory of human behavior. This theory postulates that every object created by man exists to do a job, and it is meant to do that job for a user (Dome, J. 2007). During the course of interacting with the device, the user will inevitably go through eight steps:

- define
- locate
- prepare
- confirm
- execute
- monitor
- modify
- conclude

Imagine that instead of just asking users what they think about the device, you could watch them using the device or another device to do the job before yours even exists. Imagine seeing them struggle with a particular part of the usage process, and seeing them incorporate techniques to overcome the difficulties. You could learn a lot.

Now imagine that as you watched, you observed their actions falling into each of the eight universal job steps. Imagine you recorded everything they needed to do to successfully complete each job step, and you also recorded everything they struggled with in each job step. You would learn a whole lot more about what would be needed to make your innovation successful with that user.

Techniques for Gathering Design Inputs

This is how we gather data in the discovery phase. We look through the lens of the eight job steps and record everything the device needs to do to succeed in each step, and the things that went wrong or were difficult. We use this job-step technique in ethnographies and other observational and participatory studies, but there are many ways we study and gather data in the discovery phase. Observational studies can be the most revealing, but they can be augmented with immersion techniques that put you in the shoes of the user; simulation techniques that bring users into simulated environments; and interviews, surveys, shadowing, day-in-the-life journaling, event videos, and a myriad of others.

The key that makes all of this effort worthwhile is being able to take the data you discover in your research and convert it to need statements, and eventually into the criteria that forms requirements, which the FDA calls "design inputs." We will talk about how to do this in the ethnography portion of this chapter.

It is also good to note that patent research during this discovery phase is not only good for evaluating your freedom to operate and your protection capacity and white space but is also great for generating ideas. Looking at the intricacies of what someone else has made and understanding the unique inner workings can give rise to new ideas that you may be able to capitalize on in the design of your device. This is one reason why patent research is so important in these early phases and should be done by the R&D team.

Now we will take a look at all the activities in the discovery phase. Remember that not all of these will be executed on every project. In fact, they rarely are. Consider this an arsenal that you can choose from when deciding how to get the best design research data that you can as you drive toward the goal of defining your design inputs. Here are five of the most common and important activities in this phase.

1. Investigating Intellectual Property

Time to dig in with a deeper dive into IP than in the evaluation phase. Look for design inspiration in the claims of other patents. You can also investigate expired patents or patents easily obviated in similar or related fields or functions for concept possibilities. It is also wise to search for patents making claims that you anticipate making. This helps add to your "white space" knowledge and gives you fodder for new ideas. Review a bit deeper into the patent landscape and revise your "freedom to operate" opinion if necessary, based on difficulty or likelihood as you discover more related patents and understand the current ones more deeply.

2. Assessing the Competitive Landscape

This is a good time to compile a visual and written list of competitive devices. It can be done in spreadsheet fashion, and you should rank competitive devices according to their threat level based on the criteria that you deem most important. In this spreadsheet, you can list the pros and cons of competitive devices, determine successes and failures of competitive devices with the underlying reasons, and create a list of potentially desirable features or aspects for your product from competitors based on all of the information in the spreadsheet.

3. Doing Ethnographic Research

Jane Goodall and Margaret Meade are the two most well-known ethnographers that come to mind when people talk about ethnography. They mostly worked with the tool of ethnography in an anthropological sense, studying cultures and peoples. Ethnography literally means "writing about people." *Ethno* means "people" and *graphy* means "the recording of things." With ethnographic research, you want to observe and record users employing the device or similar devices in their natural environment, recording necessary tasks (metrics) to complete each of the eight universal job steps. Then you will need to do the following:

- Identify/record pain points within the metrics, associated with each metric.
- Undergo post-observation interviews with key people and users.
- Create task analysis charts.
- Create environment and product "high touch" maps.
- Create heuristic task-analysis charts.
- Deploy user questionnaires inquiring about the necessary metrics for job steps from users.
- Deploy a user questionnaire inquiring about pain points of metrics.
- Categorize pain points into user-centric and device-centric, and create subcategories.
- Convert pain points into need statements.
- Identify unmet needs by applying an opportunity algorithm to each unmet need.
- Rank unmet needs against time, control, efficiency, safety, anxiety, and other important factors for your device.
- Create design inputs from each qualified unmet need statement.
- Enter the design inputs into the requirements document.

Now try some self-experience. You as the design engineer need to become a user in as real a setting as possible and see if you can operate the device and encounter the same pain points as the actual users. Then see if you can use the device and avoid those pain points. Evaluate: what did it take for you to avoid those pain points, and how can you get real users to do the same? This is a question you can take into your brainstorming exercises.

For access to worksheets and templates designed to facilitate these tasks, go to www.kablooe.com and lookup *templates.*

There are other types of user research that you can choose to employ during this phase as well. Some of these are:

- discussions with users and other key stakeholders
- surveys you can deploy of users and stakeholders to obtain job-step metrics and user-needs ratings
- focus groups if observed feedback on existing devices is needed but unobtainable through ethnographies; get user feedback on key questions, VOC
- blogs or other social media posts to elicit responses to key questions and observe related conversations

Aside from these activities focused on users and the actions and activities they are engaged in for your innovation, there are other areas you can explore during this discovery phase. One is a first look into human-factor issues. This involves understanding the limitations and capabilities of your selected user group in relation to their interaction with your device, and determining key user activities that might illustrate possible device shortcomings. Along with this, you will need to begin investigating anthropometrics, determining key measurements and ranges, identifying possible device function/anthropometric difficulties, and conducting a brief risk/hazard analysis related to human use.

You also want to spend time understanding the demographics of your users and key stakeholders. Can your users be grouped into any subcategories? If so, list each one and break down each group into demographic components. Then correlate important demographic data with potential design requirements

4. Determining Design Inputs and Requirements

Even before you have a defined device or prototype, it is necessary to put together a preliminary draft of early design inputs, which will drive your upcoming ideation phase and become part of your requirements document. Here are the steps you need to go through in order to do that.

- **Create a master list of user/product needs by creating need statements** resulting from all of your work done so far in the evaluation and discovery phases. This list should be in the form of need statements. Need statements are sentences that start with the phrase, "A way to ..." and then describe a need that the user has related to the use of your potential innovation.

- **Solicit user input to rank each need statement** according to importance and current satisfaction. This is done by asking users and key stakeholders to rank each need statement on a scale of 1–5 for importance (meaning how important it is to address this need) and satisfaction (meaning how satisfied they are with the current situation of addressing the need).

- **Apply the opportunity algorithm** to determine which needs will be addressed in the product design and development. This is done by simply adding to the importance number the sum of importance minus satisfaction. This value can now be assigned to each need statement. Determine which part of the need statement list will be addressed and converted to design inputs by identifying the first need statement on the list that seems to obviously be out of the scope of this project, and select all of the need statements above that one for conversion to design inputs.

- **Rewrite each of these need statements as a design input**. This is done by creating a sentence that starts with the phrase, "The device shall ..." and then completing the sentence by identifying an outcome described in general terms that is measurable in some way and would address the need from the need statement. Keep in mind that each of these design inputs will have to be evaluated and measured during your verification activities, so write them in a way that will allow you to do that.

- **Initiate the design history file (DHF)**. It is still early in the process, and a DHF is a part of your design controls, which are a requirement of your quality management system (QMS). Not to be confused with the D3 process and its phases, most manufacturers have phases in their tracking process that are indicated by numbers. Typically there is a Phase 0 which normally lines up with the Evaluation, Discovery, and Ideation phases of the D3 process. In the Design phase of the D3 process a single concept solution is identified, and this typically is the beginning of phase 1 of the manufacturers tracking process, which is initiated because you now have a concept to begin building and testing. During the D3® discovery phase, you are still in what is normally considered phase 0 of the manufacturers tracking process, and not at a point needing design controls which begin at their phase 1. However, your design inputs list can be put into your design history file even this early so that you can begin the process of building your DHF. These design inputs are a portion of your product-requirements document, which is a living document at this point and subject to change with new information.

- **Use this design input list as criteria for guidance** and a checklist for design success as development progresses.

You will need to begin to summarize other requirements that you may be able to identify with all the research done to this point. From an R&D perspective, you will start to see the formation of requirements related to design activities, such as technical and marketing requirements.

5. Assessing Limitations

Now is a good time to assess any limitations to your device or the ecosystem around your effort that may stem from inputs and requirements and identify them so they can be addressed during subsequent development phases. This could include identifying:

- items that users and key stakeholders desire to be included or excluded
- limitations potentially related to the product design
- IP limitations potentially related to the product design
- cost limitations potentially related to the product design
- corporate-strategy limitations potentially related to the product design
- other usage/environment/material limitations related to the product design.

At the end of the discovery phase, a go or no-go decision to continue to the next phase is given based on a high level of assurance coming out of the discovery activities that the value proposition is viable and sustainable, product risks are acceptable, design inputs have been defined, and requirements are being formed.

D3 Process® Phase 3: Ideation

Entering the ideation phase signifies the initiation of the activity that most designers and engineers are chomping at the bit to get to: creating concepts. Most likely, most of you who are designers and engineers have been coming up with possible concept solutions during both the evaluation and discovery phases. Hopefully, you've been logging these ideas and setting them aside to be evaluated along with the myriad of other ideas you will be coming up with in the ideation phase, and you have not fallen in love with any of them at this point.

As you launch into the ideation phase, you will need to make sure that you are setting yourself and your team up to make all ideation activities align with the design inputs established in research. This is important, because it keeps your concepts on track and prevents wasted time developing concept ideas that will not be useful to the project.

Below are several activities you will need to execute during the ideation phase, in the approximate order you'll conduct them in.

Brainstorming

Brainstorming is a great way to get started down the ideation path. You can get ideas from a large group of people in a short period of time with brainstorming, then use these ideas as springboards to develop concepts. There are hundreds of brainstorming methods you can look up and use. Some of my favorites are *reverse brainstorming* and *random juxtaposition*. Whichever methods you choose, there are some universal rules that apply:

- Have a facilitator who controls the flow of the meeting. Make sure it is a person who can maintain control of the group and has the skill to gently pull the floor away from overly controlling group members, while having a balanced-enough personality to draw the introverts into the activities.

- A couple of short sessions is better than one long one. Keep sessions to no more than forty-five minutes in length, with breaks or overnights in between.
- Use a good, open, and creative workspace. Provide supplies for idea visualization and refreshments.
- Force people to be visual with their ideas. More creative thinking occurs when people are visual instead of text-driven.
- There are no bad ideas. At least not now. Eliminate any form of criticism during the conception of and presenting of ideas. Ideas can be filtered later.
- Require participants to use "yes and ..." language when discussing concepts.
- Have a recorder list ideas as simple descriptive headlines so they can be identified later. Record any visuals that go with each idea.
- Allow time either during or after each type of brainstorming activity for participants to build on the ideas of others. This is really the most important part of brainstorming.
- Execute each brainstorming activity with positivity and energy. Energizing music can be helpful during thinking periods.
- Make sure to conduct grouping and ranking exercises after the brainstorming session, before you have forgotten the creative essence of all the concepts.
- Make sure you make the focus and purpose of the brainstorming activities clear. It is hard for participants to brainstorm on something that is vague. List your brainstorming objective on the board in the front of the room, and keep it there the entire time.

There are many things you can brainstorm on. Solutions to the main problem is the obvious thing, but that problem can usually be broken down into parts, and it may be easier to brainstorm on each of these parts. They could be things like device functionality, ergonomics, value-added features, manufacturability, and unique branding.

Once you have grouped, sorted, and ranked the concepts, feel free to throw the bad ones out. At this point, there are bad concepts. Don't be an idiot. Get rid of them. You can now begin to use concept-evaluation techniques with rankings of potential design input matching select concepts to pursue further into ideation.

Rough Sketching

Here is where the "fail smart" idea takes effect. If you were to prototype each of these concepts at this point, a lot of time and money would be spent on it. Look for ways you can most quickly and efficiently communicate the gist of the idea. Often, quick sketches can be fastest. If you can draw stick people, you can draw concept ideas with quick sketches. This also allows you to think visually and use the right lobe of your brain while you are doing it, which will boost your creative problem-solving power.

Sketches will help others understand the meat behind your concept much better than written or spoken words. People are visual thinkers, and we understand things better when we let our brain see pictures instead of words. Use 2D rough sketches to generate as many solutions to the criteria as possible.

Try to get at least eighteen versions of solutions to each area of ideation focus. If necessary, use 3D rough sketches (initial rough mock-ups) to generate solutions and support the 2D sketches, if this proves to be a more efficient way to communicate the concept details. We often call these *protocepts*. They provide a visual understanding of a concept like sketching does, and may incorporate the use of materials like duct tape, clothespins, PVC pipe, popsicle sticks, string, cardboard, paper, and play dough or modelling clay.

Concept Review

Use the sketches to conduct a concept review. Involve all stakeholders available to review the concepts. Aggregate ideas into the best possible concept solutions to move forward with, accompanied by lists of pros and cons defining how well each concept is fulfilling the items on the design input list.

Now begin to sketch the remaining ideas at a more refined level, incorporating the best features of all concepts. Develop a higher level of feature detail to fulfill the needs of functionality, ergonomics, and manufacturing in a more defined way.

Repeat the concept review, again involving as many stakeholders as possible to review the concepts. Select the concept opportunity (or opportunities) that represents the final best direction (or directions).

Mock-ups

Create rough, rudimentary mock-ups that can be seen and felt by users and stakeholders. Because you are in the ideation phase, these mock-ups should not be full-fledged working prototypes. You should still be working your way through several possible concept options, and the mock-ups should serve the purpose of helping to narrow down your options by condensing the benefits of multiple concepts into a single concept direction.

Mock-ups at this phase can also be used for investment fundraising, and it may turn out that parallel paths of effort are needed that will culminate into two different mock-ups, one focused more on the physical user interaction with the device and the other as an early feasibility bench model for testing functionality.

Early formative studies can be conducted with these mock-ups. Formative studies are a great addition to your submission to the FDA, showing that you tested your concepts with users and gathered learning that was incorporated into the device, ultimately leading to better safety and efficacy. For best results, it is a good idea to test your concepts on about eight to ten actual users, in the actual environment, or in the closest simulated environment you can manage to assemble. All of your earlier research methodologies can come into play here, making some of your studies more observational in nature, while others may be more interview-oriented.

Regardless of the form your study takes on, it is a good idea to get mock-up evaluation and input after the study from all participants and observers. Create a questionnaire and solicit input from users, marketing, R&D, sales, and corporate people as well, having them interact with the mock-ups in addition to the actual users.

Refinement

Based on input from these studies and interviews, begin to think about changes to the design, configuration and function of the device that would improve its performance against the design inputs. Create refined sketches and mock-ups and do a bit of retesting with users to see if the improvements made a difference.

Design Input Review

Once you have all of this learning under your belt, take a look at your design input list and see if any items need to change or be removed, or if new ones need to be added. You can now select and confirm the final concept direction by adjusting the design input list accordingly, and obtaining the appropriate sign-offs necessary for FDA design input review guidelines.

By the end of the ideation phase, you should have done the following:

- evaluated many concepts that all attempt to meet the demands of the design inputs
- narrowed them down to a smaller set of concepts that all have high potential
- tested these concepts with users
- down-selected again to a final single concept that incorporates all of the best possible features and attributes for meeting the demands of the design inputs

Keep in mind that even though it is a single concept at this point, it is an early concept. Technological-feasibility work is taking a parallel path to design-configuration work, and together they should both be at a point where a single approach is chosen that appears to be feasible, with the ability to meet all of the functional and user requirements. This is why your concept model at this point is not a finished working prototype and is not considered an alpha or beta unit.

Details defining tolerances for mechanical accuracy, component selection, and part details for manufacturing have not been created and implemented in the mock-ups in this phase. Your team should make considerations for these things while developing concepts to mock up, but they should not be spending time implementing these details yet. More changes will most likely be needed, and you don't want to be doing the detailed tolerance work over again and again.

At the end of ideation, preliminary concepts should have been reviewed and a concept direction agreed upon for a final configuration and approach to the design. There should also be a high potential that the design criteria can be fulfilled by the leading concept before a decision can be made to move the project into the next phase.

D3 Process® Phase 4: Design

Once a high potential concept from the ideation phase is identified and approved, you can move into the design phase of the project. The design phase is the first point at which you will be working on only one concept for your device. This can be a bit complicated, because many innovations involve more than one device; they are a system of several devices working together along with software, interface displays, and wireless communication. Each of these aspects can go through this development process on its own, including software, which has its own version of the development process.

The idea is for all of these areas to be moving forward in union, sometimes in parallel and synchronicity, other times with one waiting to go on to a next step while the other is in focused development. This is all perfectly fine. The focus in this book is much more on the device part of the innovation, specifically the parts of the device that physically interface with the human, but understand that the principles here can apply to the other areas of your innovation in many ways.

One thing people often ask about and develop some confusion over is concept iterations. They feel that if they are iterating and changing a concept they must not be using a linear process. This is not true. The development process takes into account the need for iterations and allows them in its steps. This is why you saw several rounds of sketches, mock-ups, and testing in the ideation phase. We know in advance that there will be rounds of iterations and plan for it in the linear plan.

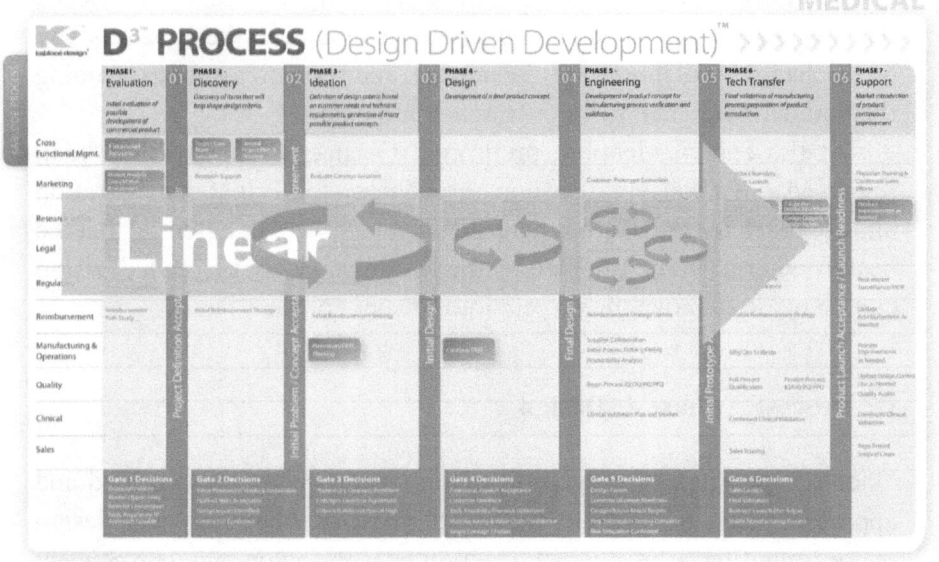

Reiterations in a linear process

I like to visualize it with several circular arrows. In the ideation phase, these arrow circles represent having a concept, learning something, then going back and changing the concept to make another. It is a design iteration. In the ideation phase, these circles are very large, representing big changes in concept thinking. In the design phase we also have these circles, but they are smaller. Why? Because we have landed on a single concept.

Design iterations now won't be focused on a complete change of concept, but rather on smaller changes within that concept. Features that the user might interface with could change in size, shape, location, or function. Methods of function could change slightly with the inclusion of a new component. These kinds of changes to the concept are smaller iteration circles, and as you continue through the process and advance to the engineering phase, the iteration circles get smaller still. Yet as they become focused on the minute details necessary for precise function and manufacturing, there are always iterations in the process. They just get more focused as you advance through development.

There are a number of major things you need to focus on in the design phase, keeping in mind that you are beginning to hone in on some of the details of a single concept in preparation for a design freeze where specifications can begin to be written. Here are eight important steps to execute in this phase.

Step 1: Concept CAD File Creation

Now is the time to build the physical parts of your device or system and create 3D CAD files that define the overall configuration, architecture, shape, and form of the product, and do it in a way that it will be useful to be transformed into engineering CAD later. At Kablooe, we have called this *concept CAD* because it is actually the start of the 3D CAD file that will be used for manufacturing, but in an early concept form.

This means that we use techniques for building parametric CAD files that will support manufacturing efforts, complete with history trees of features, mated features, and full assemblies with associated parts. Oftentimes, designers who are not focused on manufacturing or are not following a process like the D3 Process® will use a much simpler CAD program to communicate device form and part identification, but the data output from their software will not support manufacturing, and in the engineering phase the CAD files have to be remade from scratch. By using a parametric modeling software such as Solidworks from the very beginning of the design phase, we create efficiencies in the later phases.

Step 2: Final Concept Definition

This is where you begin to use concept CAD to define all areas related to the criteria list with specific feature solutions. Two parts that fit together may have just been alluded to in ideation sketches, but now you can show the shape of each part in realistic dimensions to see how it would actually look and feel. In ideation, you may have alluded to an internal roller-wheel mechanism, but now in concept CAD, you will build the wheels at their assumed actual shape and size, along with their supporting chassis member, axles, and framework. This work is done for each distinct feature of the device.

Step 3: Initial Design Risk Analysis

Once you have all of this built, it is a great time to conduct an initial design failure mode effects analysis (dFMEA) based on the CAD feature solutions that you constructed. You can use the FMEA spreadsheet that you used in the discovery phase, but here you are just focusing on design-related issues. As you fill out the spreadsheet, your final column will be a list of mitigation strategies for the design. Once this is done, make sure you make some revisions to the parts in the concept CAD files that implement the mitigation strategies into the design of the device.

Step 4: Manufacturing Review

Now you can provide concept CAD information to all involved manufacturers and solicit their opinions regarding design for manufacturing. Hopefully, you will have been using good design for manufacturing (DFM) thinking as you designed your device components and built them in concept CAD up to this point. However, each manufacturer has different needs based on specialties and the equipment they are using. Therefore, it is wise to identify who you may be using for manufacturing, assembly, and component supply and reach out to them for a review meeting of your current concept CAD files. They will be able to give you specific directions related to part and component details that will help the items move efficiently through production.

Make sure to go back and implement as many changes as possible into the concept CAD files to support their needs. You can also evaluate whether or not any of their requests create a need for revising any design inputs, and if so, make changes to that document as well.

Step 5: Concept Rendering

At this point, you are going to need to get approval from upper levels of management to move forward with this concept direction, whether your customer's or an internal team of managers and directors. You can now easily create a 3D photorealistic rendering set highlighting the important factors to all of the functional silo leaders. Sales, marketing, manufacturing, legal, etc., will all need to know what the proposed device solution is at this point and weigh in from the viewpoint of their needs on how well this solution may be meeting those needs. You should be showing them the following:

- exploded views
- component close-ups
- mated part relations
- overall look and feel
- user interface details
- packaging solutions and options
- operational details.

Make sure you have enough reviews to have the renderings seen by as many users, key stakeholders, and customer representatives as possible.

Step 6: Concept Refinement

Time to once again take what you learned from these reviews and refine the concept CAD file to create a set of final concept rendering images. Remember your iteration circles on the process chart, and embrace the activity of making changes for improvement and acceptance. If you have been building your CAD files with the correct methodology, these changes will not be hard to do and will be implementable and helpful for the manufacturing purposes.

Step 7: Initial Design Output Review

It is now a good time to take a look at your design outputs. Remember, your design inputs were a subsection of your product requirements document. The term *design inputs* is a sort of generic, umbrella term referring to those requirements that deal with user needs and product design, so often they are found in your requirements document listed as *user* (or user interface) *requirements, product requirements,* and sometimes even *marketing requirements.*

These inputs (requirements) are the things that help define what your device will be, how it will function, how it is configured, and what the user interface is like, all related to user needs. Now that you have created a device, you have made *outputs.* These are the features and unique items in your device concept that fulfill the design inputs. The FDA is going to require that you list what these outputs are, and that you demonstrate that they fulfill the inputs. This is called *design verification.*

Because this lies ahead, you now need to determine what the design outputs are. These outputs are usually listed in a specification document. The specifications define each aspect of the device that fulfills a requirement. For instance, a design requirement might be that a user cannot accidentally let go of the device handle during a phase of usage. This requirement is simple and measurable during testing. The design output might be that you have a strap in the design that must go around the user's wrist in order for the user to engage the handle.

The description of this strap is a specification within your product specification document, and a design output.

Next, you need to determine if the design inputs will match the design outputs. If you are not already convinced that they all do, another round of testing will be needed. All of the testing you have been doing to this point to help drive design iterations should be recorded as *formative studies*, complete with a written protocol and a post-study report to help support your FDA submission. Continue to evaluate, refine, and retest until you are confident that these design outputs will match and satisfy the design inputs when rigorously tested.

There is no need to get signatures or record these latest tests as an official design output review for FDA consideration. That will come later.

Step 8: Refined Mock-ups

Creating appearance model prototypes and partially functional model prototypes for user feedback and customer approval is usually all that is necessary at this point. Because you are in the design phase of the project, the prototypes are not finished—fully working prototypes that would be considered what the industry typically calls *alpha* or *beta* prototypes. These will come in the next phase; for now, you are just trying to determine if there is a good chance your users will be successful with the device and it will meet the requirements being formed. You only need to create prototypes of sufficient complexity to complete those tasks at this point.

Every prototype build and testing activity needs to have a goal. Then you can gear the effort to match the complexity of meeting that goal. If we just get prototype-happy (because we all love seeing ideas become reality) and start building complex working prototypes just because we want to, we won't be failing smart, and we could potentially be wasting valuable time and money.

The design phase is all about making sure you have a single product direction, even if it is a complex one, then refining and testing it until you and all the key stakeholders and users are confident that it is the direction you want to pursue into the next phases, where most of the time and money on the project will be spent.

After the design phase, you will need to confirm several things before moving into the engineering phase. The functional aspects of the device need to be accepted and approved by the entire project team. Customer feedback should be obtained and acted upon in the design. Technological feasibility should be proven in this phase and even planned for how it will be optimized in the design. Manufacturing and value-chain confidence should be high at this point, and the single concept should be defined in its real form and approved by the entire project team. If these items are not met, more time needs to be spent in this phase before advancing into engineering.

D3 Process® Phase 5: Engineering

Well, here you are. You are on the doorstep of the engineering phase. You have passed through all of the other phase gates, gotten approval for your concept direction, and now you are ready to dig in and make the damn thing.

The engineering phase is the largest of all phases in terms of overall spend in both time and money. This is why it is important to go through the other phases first. They lay the groundwork and give a high level of confidence that the costly work of this phase will be on target. Trust me, you don't want to do the engineering phase over. You don't even want to do parts of it over. Too costly. Fail smart, and avoid that kind of failure.

We should spend some time here discussing why we call this the *engineering* phase. Engineering can mean so many things, and there are so many kinds of engineers: mechanical, electrical, software, systems, etc. They are all responsible for different things. The reason they have the title *engineer* in common is that they all share one attribute of their disciplines: they are tasked with figuring out how to make things work. They are each doing this in the area of their own discipline.

In the spirit of this definition (which is my own interpretation), this next phase is all about figuring out how to make this thing work. Therefore, it is engineering. My personal definition of design in relation to engineering is "figuring out how to make it useful for humans." If you examine phases 2-3 of the D3 Process®, you will see that is exactly what we were focusing on.

OK, let's make sure this thing works. There are a lot of things that happen during this phase, but we will focus on twelve of the most important in the rest of this chapter.

The first thing you are tackling in the engineering phase is the functional component resolution related to all of the parts of the device that have functional aspects. Remember those wheels and frames that were part of the complex mechanical assembly that you were trying to show the feasibility of with visual renderings in the last phase? Well, you better hope that your theories of operation were at least moderately valid. Now you have to detail them out and make them work. Here you need to examine forces, tolerances, interferences, deflection amounts, thermal transfer, fluid ingress, electromagnetic interference, hold strength, and the like. Refine the parts you made in your CAD assembly to be optimized in all of these areas (and others like them).

Design Output Review

Now is the time for an official design output review. Remember the preliminary one you did in the design phase? Do it again. Only this time, do it like it is the last time you will be doing it on the project. Hopefully, it is. Basically, you are looking at the specifications of your device (yes, they should all be listed in your specification document) and making sure you are still confident that they will satisfy the requirements of your design inputs.

Component CAD File Creation

If you are fairly confident in the results of your design output review, then it is time to go even further in building out the finer details of each part and component. This can take considerable time, but you have to build each part in CAD so it can have its details refined and ready to go for complete operational success, manufacturing, and assembly.

Risk Management

Preliminary risk-management activities have been occurring throughout the early phases of the process. However, at some point, you need to start an official risk-management plan, and it can't occur any later than this phase. It could begin in the design phase, but often companies will wait until they have a design frozen with a good, testable, working prototype before they officially document this activity, feeding in information from their preliminary work in earlier phases. This is an acceptable way to approach the task.

Your risk-management plan will outline how you will assess the risks, evaluate them, and mitigate them throughout the course of the project. There are best-practice ways to do this, and from a design/usability standpoint, ISO standard 14971 does a great job of laying out the methodologies to execute risk management. As you have seen throughout the previous phases of the D3 Process®, risk-assessment thinking and activities have been occurring throughout the entire process. Keeping a good record of this information is important in order to provide a good risk-management file to the FDA in your submission.

Preliminary dFMEA 2

Another dFMEA is an important component to your risk-management plan, and a nicely documented one needs to be executed at this point in the process. We haven't explained dFMEAs in much detail yet, but since we are in the engineering phase and this one or the next might be the final one, we should talk a bit about how to do one. Design failure mode and effects analysis must be done in a stepwise fashion, since each step builds on the previous one. Here are the ten steps to a Design FMEA, as described by Quality Training Portal (FMEA Training, 2022).

STEP 1: Review the design
- Use a blueprint or schematic of the design/product to identify each component and interface.

- List each component in the FMEA table.
- If it feels like the scope is too large, it probably is. This is a good time to break the Design Failure Mode and Effects Analysis into more manageable chunks.

STEP 2: Brainstorm potential failure modes
- Review existing documentation and data for clues about all of the ways each component or interface can fail.
- Get an exhaustive list—it can be pared down and items can be combined after this initial list is generated.
- There will likely be several potential failures for each component.

STEP 3: List potential effects of each failure
- The effect is the impact the failure has on the end customer or on subsequent components.
- There will likely be more than one effect for each failure.

STEP 4: Assign Severity rankings
- Rate the severity of each effect using customized ranking scales as a guide.

STEP 5: Assign Occurrence rankings
- Determine how frequently the failure is likely to occur.

STEP 6: Assign Detection rankings
- What are the chances the failure will be detected prior to the customer finding it?

STEP 7: Calculate the Risk Priority Numbers (RPN)
- Severity × Occurrence × Detection

STEP 8: Develop the action plan
- Decide which failures will be worked on based on the Risk Priority Numbers. Focus on the highest RPNs.
- Define who will do what by when.

STEP 9: Take action
- Implement the improvements identified by your Design Failure Mode and Effects Analysis team.

STEP 10: Calculate the resulting RPN
- Re-evaluate each of the potential failures once improvements have been made and determine the impact of the improvements.

Design for Manufacturing Implementation

Now that you are happy with your risks from the failure-mode activities, it's time to focus again on manufacturing issues. By this time, you should know more about who your final manufacturing partners will be, and who your other suppliers and assemblers will be. If you are going to have field maintenance as part of your ongoing plan, you should know a bit about your field technicians' needs at this point as well. Now spend time refining all the parts in the CAD files to reflect final details related to manufacturing issues.

Manufacturing Review

Plan a meeting with the manufacturers, assemblers, and component suppliers and review the current state of the device to make sure your refinements are acceptable.

Prototype Creation

Now is the time to get deeper into prototypes and venture into alpha and beta units. An alpha prototype is the first attempt to pull everything together in a final working fashion. It doesn't necessarily mean that each part or component is in its final, manufactured form. It does mean that the functionality, interface, and usage scenario are very close if not exactly mimicking a final commercially manufactured device.

User Study

Once your alpha prototype is created, you will want to do another user study. You will again be looking to see if users can complete the tasks that the design inputs were trying to ensure, and that they operate the device safely and effectively without introducing any unexpected risk into the system.

One Last dFMEA

If unacceptable risks were still present on your previous dFMEA, you need to do a final one now. You will have new learnings from the most recent prototype and user study, and hopefully will have mitigated those lingering risks. You should now be able to refine your dFMEA to show that all risks have been appropriately mitigated.

CAD Refinements

This is an iterative process, as you have seen. You probably learned some things in that last user study that you implemented in your plan to mitigate those last few risks. You will need to go ahead and refine the parts in your CAD files to reflect these updated changes.

Refined Working Prototypes

More, really? These are the beta units. They will be used for summative testing and validation testing. If they cannot be made with all of the exact parts and materials as the commercially produced units, they have to at least use parts and materials that are so close they have no differentiating effect compared to the final commercial units on the usage of the device for the testing. These are also the units that will most likely be used for clinical trials, if such trials are necessary for your FDA submission, and are often made as a first run or a prototype run by your actual commercial manufacturer.

Design Verification and Validation

The engineering phase is when your actual verification and validation activities occur. Because this book is more about good process, and the order and inclusion of tasks in the process, we won't go into teaching methods for executing all of these tasks. We did look at evaluation and dFMEAs in a bit of depth due to their close ties with the practice of design, but verification and validation (V&V) activities have entire training courses devoted to the proper execution of these tasks. We will suffice it to say here that you should find experts in this area to help you execute these V&V tasks if you don't know how to do them yourself.

There will need to be functional V&V to make sure the device is performing according to all of its functional requirements and specifications, which includes electrical and software systems as well as any mechanical elements. Aside from these tests, you also need to perform usability validation testing where you are evaluating usability (human factors) and how well the device reaches its goals in this area.

In order to do usability validation testing, you have to conduct what is known as a *summative study*. This is a study where you are now using devices that are commercially manufactured and are the real, exact devices that actual users will be getting once sales begin. There are exceptions for using prototype substitutes, but you have to be able to make an argument that they are so close to actual commercial devices that no differences would be detected in testing.

You will need to have about fifteen to twenty separate users from each user group, and you need to test to make sure that you can document once again that all of the features of the device defined in your specifications (outputs) fulfill the user needs defined by the design/user requirements (inputs). This time, you document all of your findings in a report, and this report goes into your human factors engineering (HFE) plan file and is submitted to the FDA when you apply for approval or clearance.

With this DVT activity, you are showing that you created the right features to successfully meet those design input needs. The overall result of your validation testing for all of the other areas of the device (such as mechanical function, electronic, and software) combined is going further and showing that the device is meeting all of the user needs that were described at the beginning of the project, thus proving that your final device is the correct, intended device.

By the end of the engineering phase, you should be able to declare an official design freeze. There should be a consensus among the project team supporting commercial readiness. Verification and validation testing should be completed, and any testing to support the regulatory submission should be complete. This means the initiation of clinical trial activities fall during the end of this phase. Risk mitigation should also be completed and confirmed.

All of these items need to be checked off as complete before you move into the production phase, with the exception of the clinical trials. These trials can occur during and after the engineering phase.

D3 Process® Phase 6: Tech Transfer

The tech transfer phase is the period of time that the R&D team spends getting all the necessary information to manufacturers. Initially, this can be for quoting purposes, and then for the actual start of the manufacturing process.

For manufacturer quoting, assemblers, and suppliers will need a certain amount of information to provide cost estimates for their services. By this point, you will have already established some preliminary costs in the ideation and design phases, but these are always hard to get because manufacturers are reluctant to commit to any costs without a lot of detailed information. The tech transfer phase is all about getting them that detailed information.

This might seem like it doesn't warrant an entire phase for itself, but it really does. It takes quite a bit more time than most inexperienced developers might think. All of the latest engineering files have to be rounded up into one package with the correct version identifiers. These include the following:

- 3D CAD files for the mechanicals
- layout and schematic files for the electrical
- beta or final versions of the software and firmware files

- tech packs for any soft goods
- any tolerancing and key dimensional requirements

This can take a bit of time to put together, and then discussions need to occur with the manufacturers, allowing them to ask questions of the engineering team to more fully understand the implications that the device's unique nuances will have on their systems.

This series of information transfer and review meetings happens for several manufacturers during the quoting phase, and then once final vendors are selected, it happens again at a deeper level where more time is spent describing important details to all of the vendors.

The main goal of this phase is to make sure that design intent is preserved while the manufacturing vendors are getting all of the information they need to successfully begin their process. Most manufacturers will inevitably have suggestions to modify the device in order to more efficiently fit it into their processes. While it is good to understand these modifications and implement some of them to save time and money on part costs, an overall eye must be kept on preserving the design intent. Otherwise, a risk of introducing an opening to a previously mitigated risk or hazard could occur, or features could be compromised that negatively affect user satisfaction and desired market penetration.

At the end of the tech transfer phase, you should be ready for sales launch. All final validations should be complete, and your business launch plan should be sufficiently adjusted to support the current format of the device and the company. A stable manufacturing process should be in place, and the team should be comfortable moving into the commercial marketplace.

D3 Process® Phase 7: Support

This is final step of the D3 Process®. It begins once sufficient information has been given to the manufacturers, and they have provided a *first article* device. At this point, there may be a series of design and engineering activities that need to take place.

First of all, it may be discovered upon inspection of a first article that something needs to change. Perhaps there was an aspect of the manufacturing process that didn't repeat in production the way anticipated after prototyping. This may have caused a feature to be different than required, or some other aspect to be out of tolerance. If these things occur, the engineering team will need to go back into the CAD files and make changes to support the manufacturing anomaly.

This can be very unfortunate, and every attempt to avoid this situation should be taken in the tech transfer phase. If the change has to occur in an injection-molded part, sometimes it is relatively simple and can be executed by having the steel molds cut into a bit deeper in certain areas. This is considered a *steel safe* change. However, sometimes the change requires a steel mold to have material added back to a cavity. This is a much more time-consuming process, because new steel will have to be welded into the mold cavity and then cut away. These activities are costly in time and labor, and they push schedules out and drive costs up. The engineering team should look for as low-impact ways to solve the problem as possible, and this is part of the creative design and engineering task work in the support phase.

Other support activities can occur further down the production path. Initial market reaction might cause a change to the feature set of the product. This would be an unfortunate circumstance, but almost any need for engineering after the initial market launch is likely to be such. The support phase is really just about any activity that the design or engineering team needs to engage in to support the advancement of the company's goals with the device. New manufacturers and suppliers might need to be brought in for some reason, and design information might have to be supplied to them. This is where the design and engineering team stands ready to support, and perhaps even begins to formulate what the next-generation version of the device might be like.

This chapter has described the seven phases of the D3 Process® in some very short and general terms. For a more intricate look at all the parts and components of the process, refer to the process chart shown at the beginning of this chapter, or download a larger version of the chart at www.kablooe.com.

Chapter 13

Success Statistics

Impact on the World

Why do we do what we do? All of the things described in this book have a high level of complexity, especially if we think about medical devices and all of the regulatory hurdles and requirements. This results in a lot of hard work for everyone involved, including the design and engineering team. Why do we do it? For most of us, there is a driving force that goes beyond just the desire to use creative capabilities to create cool things. We know that the medical device we focus on, and oftentimes other types of devices as well, will improve the lives of people around the world.

In 2012, I had the privilege of being involved in a project that was making a device for young children with a rare disorder that prevented them from moving their arms. The condition these children had gave them no hope of recovery in their lifetime. A friend of mine found two inventors, an industrial designer and medical scientist, working in a lab at a hospital making 3D printed parts with rubber bands that could be worn as a low-tech exoskeleton on their arms. This device would take the tiny amount of movement that the child was able to muster and amplify it into enough movement to allow them to do important tasks of daily living, like coloring with crayons, eating, and hugging their mom.

These inventors were only able to fit one or two children a month with these devices, as they were very rudimentary, and the process to get them fit and working on a child was very complicated, time consuming, and costly. My friend Eric was moved by compassion when he found out that nearly 40,000 children around the world were suffering from this condition. After this discovery, he walked into my office and asked, "Tom, is there something we can do about this?"

I evaluated the situation and realized that the patient population, even though large in terms of human suffering, was too small to garner the interest of a company to invest in developing a device like this on a larger scale. There just would not be a return on investment for them. I told Eric that we could make a nonprofit company that could raise money and try to fund the increase of production quantities of the device, so that its distribution could reach around the world. Eric agreed, and we formed the company.

The company is still to this day working on developing the device further and getting it into the hands of parents with suffering children in remote areas of the world who don't have realistic access to clinical services. We also spun off a for-profit company, Abilitech, that developed a motorized electronic version of the device that would not only help these children but adult stroke victims and people with similar neuromuscular disorders. That device should be available to the public sometime in 2022-23.

Foundations like our local Schultz Foundation and many others are helping to fund efforts like these, enabling the creative product-design process to engage the skills and talents of designers and engineers around the world for global impact to help improve the lives of others. I can't speak for all designers and engineers, but I know that at Kablooe Design, this is why we do what we do. Improving the human condition and helping to enhance the lives of others in a positive way is the best reward possible for a creative-design professional.

Case Studies

Applying the D3 Process® can and will look very different each time it is implemented, depending on the situation and the device or system being developed. In over thirty years of product development, I have worked on many inspirational projects that have employed this process.

The following are a couple of the very effective and inspirational projects I have had the privilege to be a part of.

Anser Innovations

Getting the proper medication regimen on a regular basis is an elusive thing for millions of people each day. My wife was a nurse in an elder-care ecosystem for many years, and at one point she decided to keep track of how many patients were correctly following their medication regimen when she went to check on them in the home. After several years of tracking the accuracy of patients' medication intake versus their regimen, she asked me what I thought the percentage of accurate cases were.

I guessed 25 percent.

"No," she said.

Fifteen percent?

"No," was the answer again. "Would you believe zero percent?"

In all the years that she was the director of nursing in this system, when she checked, she never found one single patient who was ever taking medications the way their care team had prescribed.

A company called Anser Innovations decided to do something about this. It wanted to put together a device that would use a series of drive wheels and cutters to open up prepackaged pill pouches and dispense the pills into a tray that cameras would be viewing so that a remote-located caregiver could watch patients pick up the pills and actually put them in their mouth. Putting together a device like this was no small task.

Kablooe began by doing the investigations necessary to understand the needs of the users—who were patients, caregivers, pharmacists, and physicians—in the discovery phase. In the ideation phase, concepts were considered relating to the best configuration for usage, viewing, loading of medications, cutting of pill packs, operation of the feeding mechanism, and locking. In the design phase, all of these things took on a final form, and in the engineering phase, all the details were locked in to drive towards final manufacturing files.

This device is now in early-stage production and ready to be purchased in the marketplace. It will help countless users prevent overdoses and other medication-related health complications that destroy quality of life and can often be fatal.

Capital Safety

Have you ever thought about the safety of construction workers on those tall buildings? The use of a fall harness keeps them safe from fatal falls. Most fall harnesses are designed to slow a person's fall gradually, so the jerk at the end of the cable doesn't create harsh injuries. But most have to survive rough conditions with concrete and rebar abrasions, and dirt in the mechanisms. Many harnesses wear out too quickly and cause failures due to undetected wear and tear. The implications of this can be fatal.

Kablooe went through the development process and created features that helped resist the abrasion of rebar carried on the shoulders. We added ergonomic cushioning in fall stress zones, breathable moisture-wicking fabrics for comfort in heat, and features creating higher security and user convenience. The ExoFit Nex became the highest-selling fall brace in the industry, and the company was eventually purchased by 3M.

Creating innovation by driving through the process not only brought higher safety levels to improve the lives of the users but also created a high-value situation for the company to reach its acquisition goals.

NxThera

In sharing success stories, I couldn't leave out one particular start-up company example. NxThera began with a small handful of people who had a goal to treat an enlarged prostate with steam instead of the current methods of burning, freezing, radiating, or cutting. The goal was to have a procedure that took less than five minutes and could eventually be performed in an outpatient setting instead of a general surgical setting.

Oftentimes, the process for a start-up may look a bit different than a major device manufacturer due to the focus on raising various rounds of funding, and the clinical proof and working concepts required to do so. Nevertheless, we went through the process of investigating to find users' needs during many rounds of prototyping, including simple rough prototypes, all the way to intricate working models throughout the process. Many concepts were evaluated in the ideation phase, and a single concept set was focused on in the design phase, which was then more fully developed for clinical trials and commercialization.

This was a minimally invasive surgical device, and it was going to need a 510k clearance from the FDA. This meant several rounds of studies would have to be done to gather enough evidence of safety and efficacy compared to similar units on the market.

You might be wondering how or why anyone would have thought to try to create a therapy for this using steam. It is quite an interesting story. The inventor had been working on a consulting basis for a large manufacturer that was tackling the same surgery with their version of the device a few years earlier. He has some ideas to improve their device using fluids, but they didn't want to explore a version like that, and kept with their original version which used a burning technique.

He kept the idea in the back of his mind, and as his father went through a bout with prostate cancer it began to make him think about it more. He and his father built and drove racecars together, and one time when he was working on a carburetor it dawned on him that a carburetor converted vapor into energy, and he reasoned that perhaps he could use that energy to surround cells in the prostate and denature their membranes when the steam condensed to fluid. Once the membrane of the cell was denatured, it would die and be sloughed off. If he could do this to a large enough area of tissue in the prostate, he could reduce the size of an enlarged prostate, and this is how NxThera was born.

NxThera grew their team throughout the development process and had team members to handle verification and validation, risk analysis, and refinements for manufacturing. The Kablooe team had the privilege of working alongside this team and focused on the design and engineering to get all the parts successfully tested and through production.

The device was a huge success, and after successfully treating over seven thousand patients in the US and countless more in Europe and other countries, the company was acquired by Boston Scientific. This project was not only a success at drastically reducing the dangers of the process for many men and reducing life-affecting side effects, it also created great value for the company that led to the acquisition.

Projects like these are what make creative designers and engineers strengthen their drive to continue to create and help improve the lives of others. Other people are affected not only by the use of the device but also by the fact that doing development this way creates value for the company, which creates more opportunities for those companies to initiate future efforts to help people with other devices while creating jobs as those opportunities become realities. This is a great feeling to have in your work, and certainly warrants the drive to continue to design this way.

Successes

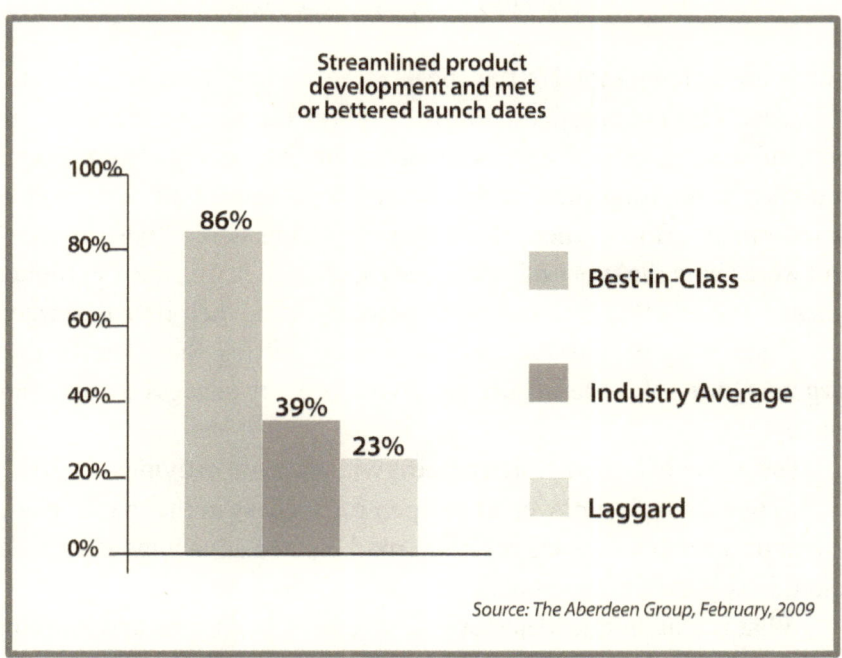

Source: The Aberdeen Group, February, 2009

Product launch timing

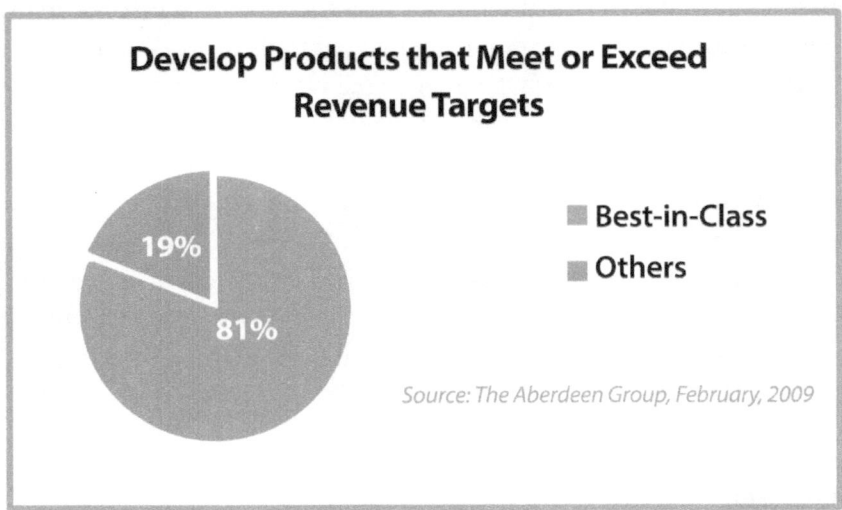

New product release revenue

There are a few statistics that bear some review here. In 2007, the Aberdeen Group compiled data from surveys to see the effect of this kind of development. The results are quite interesting. Even though statistics at the time showed that about 90 percent of all new product development efforts failed, those that were considered "best in class" and were using the types of procedures described in this book exhibited a near inverse of that figure, with 81 percent hitting their revenue targets after launching the product and 86 percent hitting their launch date targets. Quite a change in success if you measure success by time and money.

The power of a good design process with the right activities occurring at the right times is a powerful weapon for success in the marketplace. When user adoption levels are high, marketplace advantage is created, and this is good for everyone.

What is that unique idea that you have been pondering and thinking of developing? Is there some device on your mind? Perhaps an app, an environment, a system of some sort, or another type of innovative product? The ideas and techniques in this book have given you more than enough information to start. Be brave, be bold, and be a seeker looking for information and wisdom from all sources around you. Then launch out, and with the tools from this book in your tool belt you will be equipped and ready to hit the trail and forge ahead on a new path of innovative discovery.

Good luck, and you can do it!

The process of discovery involved in creating something new appears to be one of the most enjoyable activities any human can be involved in.—Mihaly Czikszentmihalyi

References

Anthony, S. D. (2021, April 14). Making Innovation an Everyday Habit in Your Organization. *Harvard Business Review,* Innovation.

Association for Psychological Science. 2010. "A Positive Mood Allows Your Brain to Think More Creatively." http://www.psychologicalscience.org/index.php/news/releases/a-positive-mood-allows-your-brain-to-think-more-creatively.html.

Barba-Sánchez, V. 2019. "Book Review: *Transformational Entrepreneurship." International Journal of Entrepreneurship and Innovation*, 20 (1): 72–73, https://doi.org/10.1177/1465750319826860.

Beaty, Roger E., et al. 2018. "Robust Prediction of Individual Creative Ability from Brain Functional Connectivity." *Proceedings of the National Academy of Sciences* 115 (5): 1087–1092. https://doi.org/10.1073/pnas.1713532115.

Brown, T. (2009) *Design Thinking Defined.* IDEO Design Thinking. https://designthinking.ideo.com/

Corse, P. 2009. "Marketing Principles for New Product Developers." Kellogg School of Global Marketing, Chicago, April 2009.

Czikszentmihalyi, M. 2009. "Creativity: Flow and the Psychology of Discovery and Invention." Kindle Edition, 466. Harper Collins ebooks.

Dictionary.com (2022, May 5) *Human Engineering.* Dictionary.com. https://www.dictionary.com/browse/human-engineering

Dome, J. 2016. "Jobs-to-be-Done: Learn and Apply the Framework." *Strategyn*, July 22. https://strategyn.com/jobs-to-be-done/#Theoryrobinm_0768f3dr.

Doré, B. P., R. R. Morris, D. A. Burr, R. W. Picard, and K. N. Ochsner. 2017. "Helping Others Regulate Emotion Predicts Increased Regulation of One's Own Emotions and Decreased Symptoms of Depression." *Personality and Social Psychology Bulletin* 43 (5): 729–739. https://doi.org/10.1177/0146167217695558.

Duncan, J. 1984. "Selective attention and the organization of visual information." *Journal of Experimental Psychology: General, 113*(4), 501–517. https://doi.org/10.1037/0096-3445.113.4.501

Dziersk, M. 2010. "Visual Thinking: A Leadership Strategy." *Design Management Review* 18 (4): 42–49. https://doi.org/10.1111/j.1948-7169.2007.tb00093.x.

Erickson, Peter. 2009. "Innovating on Innovation." Front End of Innovation Conference, Boston.

Fredrickson, B. L. 1998. "What Good Are Positive Emotions?" *Review of General Psychology* 2 (3): 300–319. https://doi.org/10.1037/1089-2680.2.3.300.

Fredrickson, B. L. 2001. "The Role of Positive Emotions in Positive Psychology: The Broaden-and-Build Theory of Positive Emotions." *American Psychologist* 56 (3): 218–226. https://doi.org/10.1037/0003-066x.56.3.218.

Fredrickson, B. L., M. M. Tugade, C. E. Waugh, and G. R. Larkin. 2003. "What Good Are Positive Emotions in Crisis? A Prospective Study of Resilience and Emotions Following the Terrorist Attacks on the United States on September 11th, 2001." *Journal of Personality and Social Psychology* 84 (2): 365–376. https://doi.org/10.1037/0022-3514.84.2.365.

Fredrickson, Barbara. 2003. "The Value of Positive Emotions." *American Scientist* 91 (4): 330. https://doi.org/10.1511/2003.4.330.

Fry, A. 2009. "The Post-it Note Was Not an Accident." Design of Medical Devices Conference, Minneapolis.

Harris, J. B. 2004. "Neurotoxicology: What the Neurologist Needs to Know." *Journal of Neurology, Neurosurgery & Psychiatry*, 75, suppl_3: iii29–iii34. https://doi.org/10.1136/jnnp.2004.046318.

Interaction Design Foundation. 2017. "What is Visual Perception?" https://www.interaction-design.org/literature/topics/visual-perception.

King, B. 2016. *The Laughing Cure: Emotional and Physical Healing—A Comedian Reveals Why Laughter Really Is the Best Medicine*. New York: Skyhorse Publishing.

King James Bible. 2017. King James Bible Online. https://www.kingjamesbibleonline.org/. (Original work published 1769.)

Kudrowitz, B. M., and Wallace, D. R. 2010. "The Play Pyramid: A Play Classification and Ideation Tool for Toy Design." *International Journal of Arts and Technology* 3 (1): 36. https://doi.org/10.1504/ijart.2010.030492.

Lekhi, Manoj. n.d. "The 95%–5% PRINCIPLE." Accessed February 28, 2022. https://manojlekhi.in/the-95-5-principle-3/.

Linehan, J., Ph.D., E. Pate-Cornell, E. M.D., P. Yock, M.D., and J. Pietzsch, Ph.D. 2007. "A Study and Model of the Device Development Process." Technical Report, the Institute for Health Technology Studies.

Mayo Clinic. 2016. "Slide Show: How Your Brain Works." https://www.mayoclinic.org/brain/sls-20077047?s=5.

Merriam-Webster. (n.d.). Gestalt. In *Merriam-Webster.com dictionary*. Retrieved May 15, 2022, from https://www.merriam-webster.com/dictionary/gestalt

Mindfulness Exercises. 2017. "417 Hz Wipes Out All the Negative Energy." https://mindfulnessexercises.com/417-hz-wipes-negative-energy/.

National Center for Education Statistics. 2013. "A First Look: 2013 Mathematics and Reading: National Assessment of Educational Progress at Grades 4 and 8." https://nces.ed.gov/nationsreportcard/subject/publications/main2013/pdf/2014451.pdf.

Post, S. G. 2005. "Altruism, Happiness, and Health: It's Good to Be Good." *International Journal of Behavioral Medicine* 12 (2): 66–77. https://doi.org/10.1207/s15327558ijbm1202_4.

Preidt, Robert. n.d. "Study Challenges Theory About Left Brain/ Right Brain Behavior." WebMD. https://www.webmd.com/mental-health/news/20130815/study-challenges-theory-about-left-brainright-brain-behavior.

Resource Engineering, Inc., n.d. "10 Steps to Doing a Design FMEA." FMEA Training. https://fmea-training.com/10-steps-design-failure-mode-and-effects-analysis/.

Robinson, K. 2006. "Do Schools Kill Creativity?" TED Talks, February. https://www.ted.com/talks/sir_ken_robinson_do_schools_kill_creativity.

Sawhney, M., & Wolcott, R. C. (2004). The seven myths of innovation. *Financial Times*.

Soon, A. (2013, March 22) *Dr. Geoff Nicholson, the "Father of Post-it Notes", on 3M and Innovation.* Hardware Zone. https://www.hardwarezone.com.sg/feature-dr-geoff-nicholson-father-post-it-notes-3m-innovation

Thomas, A. P. 2014. *Making Makers: Kids, Tools, and the Future of Innovation.* Minneapolis: Make Community, LLC.

TO112 Expert. 2020. "The Power Of Sound: 528 Hz." *TO112*, January 31. https://www.to112.com/blogs/news/the-power-of-sound-528hz.

Wikipedia. 2021, "Design Research." https://en.wikipedia.org/wiki/Design_thinking

Wikipedia (2022, March 27) *Design Thinking.* Wikipedia. https://en.wikipedia.org/wiki/Design_thinking

Wikipedia. 2022 "Semantics." https://en.wikipedia.org/wiki/Semantics

Wikipedia. 2022. "Visual Cortex." https://en.wikipedia.org/wiki/Visual_cortex.